Rainbows in the Valley

By, Cindi Tucker

I want to dedicate this book to Bill, my husband of thirty eight years, and my two daughters Leigh Ann and Meredith. Without their unwavering love and support I would not have written about this chapter in my life. They continue to bring much joy and fulfillment to my life. Through their lives they exemplify the love of Christ to those they love and serve. I am truly blessed, exceedingly abundantly above all that I could have ever imagined.

Table of Contents

Chapter One – God Called Us 7

Chapter Two – Building Serenity Valley 15

Chapter Three – Daily Life..25

Chapter Four – Taking Up Our Cross Daily..32

Chapter Five – Listen, Listen, Love, Love 43

Chapter Six – Jesus Was With Him...49

Chapter Seven – Wrapped in the Lord..53

Chapter Eight – A Family Ministry 66

Chapter Nine – Fences Around the Pasture...70

Chapter Ten – Support From Others 77

Chapter Eleven – Camel Kisses 82

Chapter Twelve – Daughters to the King of Kings....................................89

Chapter Thirteen – Love and Tears...93

Chapter Fourteen – Oh So High A Price 103

Chapter Fifteen – Life after Serenity Valley...109

Appendix..118

* Some names and identifying details have been changed to protect the privacy of individuals and organizations.

Chapter One – God Called Us

¹I will lift up mine eyes unto the hills, from whence cometh my help.

² My help cometh from the LORD, which made heaven and earth.

³ He will not suffer thy foot to be moved: he that keepeth thee will not slumber.

⁴ Behold, he that keepeth Israel shall neither slumber nor sleep.

⁵ The LORD is thy keeper: the LORD is thy shade upon thy right hand.

⁶ The sun shall not smite thee by day, nor the moon by night.

⁷ The LORD shall preserve thee from all evil: he shall preserve thy soul.

⁸ The LORD shall preserve thy going out and thy coming in from this time forth, and even for evermore. - Psalms 121

It was the first week of January 2006 when we left for Serenity Valley Ranch, the day dawned cold and cloudy. We had packed up the house, and were drinking coffee as our church family from Grace Church in Gladstone began to arrive. Bill's family was already there helping us as well, and his brother Tom took over inside the truck to see to it that it was packed tightly. Before we knew it there were so many of our friends and loved ones there cheering us on and loving on us that we lost count. It was a celebration of our call to serve Christ in Arkansas. We were humbled by the whole process as we laughed and tripped over each other until the task was accomplished. Holding hands we prayed together and hugged each other with tears in our eyes. We had lived in the Upper Peninsula of Michigan for many years and these dear folks were our support system for what lay ahead of us in the years to come. God was there and He was pleased I am sure by the love that exists in His name.

This was to become a journey that would forever change our lives. We were about to learn that the God we serve shows up in a bigger and more powerful ways than we had ever experienced before. We were also going to experience the deceit and pain, and destruction that only the evil one can bring. On this day however, we were excited and happy to be finally going.

Bill had worked for Alger Delta for nearly 25 years and he had risen to the position of General Manager. I had raised our two beautiful daughters, and taught piano lessons in our community for 26 years. Our decision to leave our life behind in Michigan and move to Arkansas was not entered into lightly. In March of 2005 our daughter Leigh Ann was working as an RI (Resident Instructor) at Rawhide Boys Ranch in New London, Wisconsin. Meredith was working at Silver Birch Ranch as a Retreat Coordinator. They had come home for Easter and were talking to us about the lives they were leading at their respective ministries. Meredith's heart was for missions and Leigh Ann loved working with the guys at Rawhide. Bill mentioned he felt sad for all the lost potential in our prisons, because they did not know Christ as young men.

They had to end up in prison before they saw their need for the Lord Jesus Christ. He and I had served on the staff of a ministry called Kairos, then Michigan Keryx, as well as being volunteers for Prison Fellowship. We were so blessed to serve in the maximum security prison at Marquette Branch prison for about seven years then in the Trustee Division for six more. Leigh then said to us, "Mom and Dad if you want to make a difference in the lives of kids you should become house parents!" That comment would change our lives forever. My first inclination was to say no way! I have already raised my kids and worked with hundreds of others in music programs and at church. I love kids and so does Bill! However that was a horse of a different color. Working with at risk kids is like no other thing you will ever do in your whole life.

The girls returned to Wisconsin and the idea began to germinate in our hearts. Bill was at the top of his company and could coast on out to retirement. We had a wonderful church family, dynamic pastor teacher, comfortable home, and wonderful friends and family close by. Why would be uproot our lives now? I was forty nine and Bill had just turned fifty. We were in good health and enjoyed our freedom as the girls were no longer living at home. I remember journaling about this discussion and praying for God to give us clarity and wisdom, before we went any further. We had never heard of Stormharbor and knew no one in Arkansas. However God can do whatever He wants and we were to make their acquaintance very soon. We had listened to and studied with the Pastor from a church in Houston Texas called Barachah. We had found his teaching from the Greek and Hebrew brought the scriptures alive to us. We were also very busy at Grace Church and loved the blessings of serving side by side with those great folks. I digress... in the box of tapes from Barachah was a bulletin from a Sunday service. In it was a list of the ministries they supported among them being the name Stormharbor Youth Ranch. This caught our attention. We began to discuss what it would mean to do this type of ministry and how it would work. We prayed about it and prayed some more. The idea just would not leave us alone. Working with kids had always been a source of great joy to me. Bill was enlivened when we had kids around. We were still young enough to keep up with them, and the idea of being able to pour the love of Christ into them was all consuming. I arrived at the decision before Bill. I knew that I must be silent and that he would have bring it up to me first.

On a Sunday morning in church at Grace, a young woman we had known for some time got up to tell about her missions trip to Africa. She was calm and confident, as well as teary. She shared how God had worked in her life during that time in Africa, how she often did not get to enter the villages they were hoping to go to because the Muslims would kill the Christians if they did. She spoke of prayer-walking in the desert and knowing God would use that power for their good and His glory. Bill was tearful after the service and turned to me and said "Cindi if she can go to Africa, I can go to Arkansas". We were to take one more jaunt before all is said and done. Having made the decision to house parent we went to Rawhide Boys Ranch to see if they needed any house parents there. We toured and talked to house parents there but they did not have any openings at that time.

We went home with a resolve. I contacted Stormharbor by email and heard back right away from Dustin, the director at that time, of Stormharbor Youth Ranch. He wanted to talk to us by phone and so we set up a time. He sent us applications and all kinds of information about the Ranch as well as intimated he had something exciting to discuss with us. We made the call and were encouraged that we might just be heading in the right direction. We communicated back and forth and finally set a date to go to Arkansas and interview. We found out that just recently a wealthy couple had given Stormharbor the money to purchase Serenity Valley Ranch. It is situated 7 miles away from the current campus and the plan was to open it up as a facility for at risk teenage girls, as on the current campus of Stormharbor they had served only boys. We had been keeping our girls in the loop and invited them to go to Arkansas with us for the interview process. We were not able to get away until the end of June. At that time it is really hot in Arkansas!

We had a wonderful time on that trip with our girls. They had grown up to be beautiful women and we laughed and talked the miles away. We could not know all that God had in store for them and for us. By then they had both met their future husbands, although they did not know that things would turn out that way. How neat it is to rear children who actively seek to follow and serve the Lord Jesus Christ. They were so very loving and supportive to us both in this process and we could not imagine being so far away from them both, as we would be if we went to the Ranch.

We arrived at the Ranch at lunch time and were greeted warmly by everyone we met. We would settle in to a mobile home set up for guests. Mrs. Jackie was tooling around on her golf cart and stopped us as we were out walking around. She was gracious and kind in her welcome. I was to find out later that she made the "best sweet tea" in all of Arkansas. The boys on Ranch loved it when she would share some of her liquid gold! Our interview would last a whole day. We found out that they were hoping we would be the ones to get Serenity Valley in shape and ready to take girls by August of 2006. We spent a great deal of time with the senior staff and were thoroughly questioned on what we believed in and how we would handle certain situations. It seemed to please them when we said we were ready willing and able to learn what we needed to know in order to be the best ranch parents we could be. We were assured that we would house parent for a few years then actively take over the administration of the girl's ranch and any new homes that would be built there. With Bill's background in management we believed that would be a great asset for the future of Serenity Valley.

The average time a house parent lasts at facilities for at risk kids is about 18 months. Little did we know what we were to learn in the years to come, and how it would change and shape us for the remainder of our lives.

One of my favorite memories was being taken to Serenity Valley to tour the ranch. You turn off a dirt road that runs through the Ouachita National forest and wind your way down into the valley. I had such a peace as we pulled onto the property. I could see girls there, playing or sitting on the big wide front porch of the Lodge. I saw beautiful flower beds and flowering trees. We walked into the building that would house the girls and I fell in love with the great room and fire place. I just knew that we were meant to be there. There was much work that needed doing before we could take our first girls and we had not yet been formally hired to work there.

We left for home in a few days with a promise to pray and pray some more about whether we were supposed to be there. They would be doing the same thing. We would give them our answer early in August. We all arrived at the same conclusion and knew we were headed to Arkansas.

Alger Delta now had to initiate a search to replace Bill as General Manger, and that would take five months to complete. I worked with other piano teachers in the area to find placement for all my piano students. We began to weed out the accumulation of stuff that had overtaken our home and garage and yard. It was a joyful time of expectation. We worked hard and long to get to the place where we were ready to leave for Serenity Valley.

On a Sunday morning late in the year Pastor Steve asked us to share about the ministry God had called us to in Arkansas. Meredith and I sang together on that Sunday and the girls shared in the tears as well. We were saying good bye to our church family. The deacons and elders and whoever else wanted to lay hands on us and prayed the power of God over the ministry we would help to start. Afterwards there was a pot luck dinner and we talked until we were hoarse. The love there was palpable and it has not changed all these years later. We are blessed beyond our wildest comprehension by those good folks and we know it! We knew that we had committed to Stormharbor and were all in!

Now it was full steam ahead getting ready to leave in early January of 2006. It is hard to believe we began this process back in March. We had our last Christmas at the house on 29th Lane. The girls both brought guys home to meet us at that time. Amos Anderson and Jeffrey Rice. Both would become our sons in love in the months to come. Leigh Ann and Jeff met at Rawhide and married in Sheboygan, Wisconsin the 29th of April 2006. Meredith and Amos met at Rawhide as Amos was the other RI in the house Leigh Ann was working in. They would marry July 22, 2006 in St Paul, Minnesota. We love these men and believe God kept our girls just for them. This made leaving them behind easier as we knew that they were well loved and cared for.

One piece of advice we were given at Stormharbor, was to take a second honeymoon and enjoy quiet time together before we came, as once we got there we would be in a whirlwind to get things ready to take in girls. We went to the Chanticleer on the Door Peninsula of Wisconsin. It was a cabin in the woods and had everything you needed to be isolated and comfortable. After that we went to Rawhide to spend time with Leigh Ann and the boys who stayed there for Christmas. Before we knew it we were packing the truck to leave for Arkansas.

What a whirlwind week it was tying up loose ends and saying good byes to family and friends. Many tears, and yet such anticipation of what God had called us to. We had set our faces for Serenity Valley, and knew that God would go before us. We stayed the night in a hotel in Escanaba before we packed the truck. We both fell into bed exhausted and yet our minds were racing. Early the next morning we got up to go pick up the truck, I was concerned that our stuff would not all fit in the size that we ordered, so after talking with the gentleman at the garage we were given the biggest one they make and it turned out that the truck he had was very new as well. He did not charge us the difference and we were humbled that he was so gracious. Back home to pack and leave that day for Serenity Valley. The ride in the truck was a sweet time for Bill and me. We talked about the Lord's leading and how everything has worked out for us to go. We talked about our daughters and how much we are going to miss having them in our lives. Yet each was independent and serving Christ in her life, therefore we knew He would care for them. Our hopes and dreams for this ministry we were going to start, as well as our feelings of being unsure what to do for them. All in all the trip was sweet and entirely too fast. Driving that big truck across I-40 being buffeted by the passing semi-trucks was a thrill ride, as well as driving through the mountains was a test of our prayer life. The sweetest moment was driving down the Stormharbor road and coming into Shiloh Valley, seeing the white fences that corralled the horses and cows and all the beauty that surrounded it. We are here!!!!!!!!!!

Chapter Two – Building Serenity Valley

We had lots of snow that winter and the scenery was lovely and white. We got to Arkansas and it was like fall again! That would last the whole winter and then there was spring. I was enamored with the country side and all the things that grew there that I had never heard about before. I was blessed to have a lady who was a long time resident of the area come over to the Ranch and tell me what would grow there and what would not. Right away I bought pansies and planted them in a bed in my front yard. Imagine flowers in the winter time! I knew that I would love making and filling flowers beds there, and I was right. Crape Myrtle trees at that time of year look like sticks sticking up out of the ground. However mid-June they start to flower and flower the rest of the summer into the fall. So many glorious colors to choose from. We eventually lined the circle drive at the Lodge with every color available. It was a beautiful sight when you drove into the valley to see all the color.

We would eventually move into the bunk house which was across the lawn from the Lodge. We would sleep there nights so that there was not a man in the house when the girls were sleeping. We were told and understood that this would protect Bill as well as comfort the girls. We had accepted this and worked diligently to clean the bunk house of all the dead critters and dust that had accumulated from long years of non-use. In the meantime we were sleeping upstairs in the Lodge. This property was used for some very interesting things one of which was a "Dude Ranch". Just before we came it had been a retreat for churches and pastors. This theme would reappear in our lives in the years to come.

We had a day off and decided to go on a picnic on Mt Ola, there were picnic tables and a view that was amazing. As we were driving there a bug hit our windshield and we both just laughed right out loud, as we had never seen bugs in January in the Upper Peninsula of Michigan. We could honestly say we were in a foreign country and were to find out that even though we all spoke English we actually spoke a foreign language as well. We were used to being told we had an accent and folks would stop and say they knew we were not from around those parts. It was all true and sometimes it was done in a hurtful way. We were to learn that there is no easy way to be accepted and sometimes you never were. Yankees were not welcomed in a lot of places in the South and we were not going to be the exception.

The first week we were there we met our first "neighbor" we would later name him Bartlett as he was fond of the pears on our trees. He was a beat up old horse who belonged to a neighbor. He would regularly get out of his fence and come for a snack. We would throw a rope over him and lead him home again. I found him standing on our front porch and we just decided that we would probably see him again and again. We were right!

The first night the water went off. We had to call for help and Scooter came over and primed the pump and got it started again. There was much that needed doing before we could begin the work there. There were electrical issues, plumbing issues. The need for beds and bedding, and getting the kitchen set up for feeding up to twelve folks, or more as the case may be. However we were enlisted right away as relief house parents for the boy's ranch house parents who had waited for us to come so that they could have some well-deserved time off. We were asked to work in the class room where the elementary boys were. Miss Susan was an amazing teacher but her father was slowly leaving this earth and she was called often to travel to his bed side. We were so tired by the end of the day that the list for Serenity Valley did not get anything removed from it.

We got to June first and we approached Dustin and urged him to let us work at Serenity Valley as they had set the date of August 1st to begin taking girls. However the kids were getting ready to go to camp and we were at one of the boy's houses taking care of them while their house parents were gone for a week. We then went to camp. I had some fun with the guys getting them packed and ready for camp. One of the boys was struggling to get his suitcase packed and shut and came to me for help. I asked how much underwear he had packed and he said he had packed six pairs. I stood there scratching my head and asked him why he thought he would need six pairs. He said they were going to be gone five days and he wanted on extra pair incase. I informed him he could take three pair and just turn them inside out and backwards. To which he then looked at me in bewilderment, and we both started to laugh! I was kidding of course and later taught him how to roll things to make them fit. He was a sweet kid and we would later develop a deeper friendship with him. We loved the fellowship and teaching that happened at camp and it built us up for the task ahead.

Determined to get things accomplished we pushed ahead with preparations for the opening of Serenity Valley. A wonderful lady whose husband was on the board of directors undertook to buy the bedding for the girl's beds. Folks donated bunk beds and dressers and we started setting up each room with love and prayer. Folks from our home church in Michigan came and rewired the Lodge and put in a new panel for us. Folks from a church in Little Rock came out and in one day painted the inside of the Lodge and the whole outside of the bunkhouse. Anita who would become our first RI came and painted the front porch of the Lodge. I have always loved porches so I began collecting and buying rockers for the porch so that we could sit and rock and take in the quiet beauty. Bill made flower beds for me in front of the bunkhouse and I planted roses and azaleas. I put over two hundred bulbs in the gardens that fall so that there would be beautiful flowers in the spring. Every color of tulip, hyacinth, crocus, and lilies. We had a group of women from a church in Nebraska come and help me rip out the monkey grass from the beds in front of the Lodge and plant every color of day lily. They were troopers as we had red ant in those beds and had to kill them before they took over. We put flower boxes on the railings at the Lodge and built railings at the bunkhouse for the same reason. I don't know if I can tell you all the ways we worked to beautify and clean up the property in preparation for the girls to come. It was a labor of love.

Another wonderful thing that happened in that time period was that both our girls would get engaged and then married in that first year we were in Arkansas. Jeff Rice and Amos Anderson joined our crazy family, and we were so happy to have them. Later in that same year they would all answer a call to come on staff at Stormharbor as teachers. We could not have foreseen that event happening but we believed God knew we would need all the support and love we could get! God showed up in a big way and gave us back our family! We are so humbled by His grace and mercy.

Lord, I have heard of your fame; I stand in awe of your deeds. O Lord. Renew them in our day, in our time make them known; in wrath remember mercy. - Habakkuk 3:2

The summer flew by and we went to training in Dallas held by the Southwest Association of Christian Homes for Children. We learned so much those few days about what it was going to take to provide a safe and loving environment for girls. What it was going to cost us personally and spiritually to be involved in the healing process that would take place. I was a bit overwhelmed however my resolve was steady as was Bill's. We had yet to begin to understand the depth of the wounds that these girls were bringing into Serenity Valley. That would become apparent as we began taking girls. We were excited as much had been done to ready the facility for the arrival of our kids and we were impatient to begin providing a safe and secure place for the girls to come to and heal. However we had one more event planned for Serenity Valley before the official start-up date. We were hosting a ladies retreat for all the ladies on the Ranch. Both young and old staffers and daughters were invited to come and fellowship and eat and laugh. We were so blessed that many came and stayed the night there with us and celebrated the opening up of Serenity Valley. Mrs. Maggie was our devotions leader and she did a wonderful job. I learned that Maggie had walked a long and difficult road and yet has loved and served Christ all the way. John and Maggie have served at Stormharbor by that time, over fifteen years. They retired and bought a mobile home and placed it on the property. John taught wood shop and Maggie taught countless young men how to read. They are part of the reason why Stormharbor exists. They love kids and prove it every day of their lives. We wrapped things up and cleaned up then it was Sunday and we went to church.

    We had begun attending a small church in Hot Springs. There was a young pastor there who was on fire for Christ and a scholar of the Word of God. We were fed spiritually there, and the fellowship was sweet. They had a connection to the Ranch and so we were with folks who loved and cared for us and the kids we were to serve. We would attend this church for most of the time we were at the Ranch. We experienced great periods of spiritual growth and great periods of trials. We knew they were praying and supporting us. This church was almost fifty miles away from the Ranch. The road there was highway 7 and it was a twisting and turning nightmare, especially when there were ice storms or rain storms. We would traverse this road numerous times as it was the road that the two Ranches were on. I became adept at keeping our fifteen passenger van on this road in spite of nature's best efforts to the contrary. One of our RI's would get car sick so we took turns driving as when she was driving she did not get sick.

    There was a brief period of time when the funds were tight and we were told to attend church closer so we attended First Baptist Church of Perryville. They were sweet and loving folks there as well. It was a shorted drive only about a half hour or so. We would eventually go back to Hot Springs and attended there until we left the Ranch.

August 5th was the official start-up date for Serenity Valley and we took our first girl very close to that time. The Ranch had a friend in the Juvenile Division in Harrison, Arkansas. Mrs. Tara was a friend to kids who were in trouble. She would funnel many kids to Stormharbor over the years we were at Serenity Valley and our first girl was from that area. She would come to know Christ at Serenity Valley, I was blessed to be the one to lead her to Him. She brought laughter and stories and love to our home and we knew that she had much to over-come. God blessed us for having known her and eventually we would reconnect with her and are still in touch with her today. She is happily married and has two kids.

We added two more girls right away. One from the Harrison area and one from out of state. As we added more girls of course the drama would go up in the house. Each girl brought her own hurt and pain. Each would bring laughter and love as well. We were to keep one girl at the Ranch until she graduated from High School. The other ran away once and we brought her back however she ran away again and we had to let her go. When she ran away the first time it was devastating to Bill and me.

We lived in the Ouachita National Forrest and it was dangerous to run away into the woods. We were scared and upset and called for back-up help from the other Ranch. They had cooler heads than we did, they called the Sheriff and thus began the hours of looking by four wheeler, cars and trucks and every other available vehicle. She was eventually found having gotten a ride across Lake Nimrod with a fisherman who then called the police. She was returned unharmed. We were relieved and received her back like the Prodigal's Son. She would stay another year or so then leave. She would come back to us one more time, she ran again and we had to let her go. So many times the things driving these young women were deep in their souls and would take years to surface and be worked through. Some never address their hurt and pain and so will run for the rest of their lives in some form or fashion. We were to get to the place that when a new girl came to live at

Serenity Valley we would give her direction to turn left at the end of the driveway so that they would end up in civilization instead of going deeper into the forest. We would give them a pep talk about the poisonous snakes, spiders, bears, bobcats, and other such critters that called the forest their home, and they did not like intruders. Maybe a mild scare of this sort would give the girls cause to pause, and rethink running away. I would often tell the girls, "wherever you go there you are." Meaning they could run away but the troubles in their hearts and lives would travel right along with them. Only Jesus Christ could bring healing and peace to their hearts and lives.

The Spirit of the Sovereign Lord is on me, because the Lord has anointed me to preach good new to the poor. He has sent me to bind up the brokenhearted to proclaim freedom for the captives and release from darkness for the prisoners... - Isaiah 61:1

They did not understand at first but over the days and weeks that they would live with us we would tell of Jesus Christ and His healing powers. That He alone could set them free from the hurt and pain in this world.

Bill and I both know the pain of abuse, and so we can with hearts filled with love, council these girls toward the only thing that will bring healing and peace. Christ Jesus and Him alone will set the captives free, and bind up their broken hearts.

This theme would run through all we did and said to those kids during the years we were to serve there. I would walk through the valley of healing during our time there as would Bill. Committed to Freedom would play a huge roll in that process. We both attended retreat weekend for that ministry and there found the tools to work through our pain and then apply the same scriptures and techniques to lead the girls through when they were ready.

The Lord always provided what we needed right on time. I spent many nights listening to stories of abuse and pain and hugging girls while they cried out their hurt and pain and anger. I know a God who is bigger than the evil one of this world and day by day He would restore the broken places in the hearts and lives of these girls. The evil one fought very hard against us in that valley, he is not willing to give back any territory that he has claimed as his own. However we saw over and over the power of the resurrection of Jesus Christ to take back these girls lives and set their face toward God. I put scripture verses on the walls of the Lodge and in the halls and even in their rooms.

The word of God is alive and powerful sharper than any two edged sword piercing asunder the soul and the spirit the joints and the marrow and is a critic of the thoughts and intents of the heart, - Hebrews 4:12

Glory to God for His powerful word which can bring power and healing in the lives of our girls and in our own. The journey was just beginning, we would see many lives touched and transformed both the boys and girls we served and in the volunteers that would come to help us. God shows up!

"Though the mountains be shaken and the hills be removed, yet my unfailing love for you will not be shaken nor my covenant of peace be removed." Says the Lord, who has compassion on you. - Isaiah 54:10

Holding onto the scriptures and having it present in our home was a way of placing the promises of God deep into their hearts. Each morning we would have devotions with the girls before they left for school. We would often have a straggler, and would have to go upstairs to hurry them along with getting ready. Teaching them to respond to an alarm clock often posed problems. I would have to resort to extraordinary measures to get them to rise on time. I have been known to hide alarm clocks around their rooms each set for the time to get up. I have sang, pounded pots and pans, and even used a wash rag with cold water to wipe their faces to rouse them. Needless to say I did not find favor with the girl who needed this extra encouragement but eventually they realized it was much more peaceful if they would get themselves up and not leave it to me.

Those early days were filled with learning what to do and not to do when taking care of these kids. We found it would take six months to a year for the girls to completely trust us and find acceptance in their placement. We had some short periods of time, others we would have for longer. Each was unique and had special talents that they brought to the table at Serenity Valley. One thing Bill and I insisted on was having a family dinner time. Each night we would all sit down together and eat and talk about what happened during their day. Each had a voice and was listened to as if they were the only one there. We had arguments which I put a stop to and would address after dinner. We laughed, and celebrated birthdays, good grades, promotions, and all the good stuff that happened to them. We always served our meals buffet style as there were often so many at the table we would be passing and not getting to eat while the food was hot. Each was required to be present and we had to by law to make a well balanced meal available however we could not force them to eat. Food quite often was used as a power tool and we had to diffuse that right away. Bill devised a method of putting a stop to the mealtime battles. He made up meal cards and each girl got two. They could for any dinner meal present us with the card and go make herself a sandwich. However at the end of the month if we did not get any cards back we would take them all out for a pizza party. From the day they got their first cards until we left we never received a meal card back. The girls encouraged each other to eat what was in front of them. We did however go through great volumes of catsup and Ranch dressing!

One of the other ways we began to teach them responsibility was to have a chore board. They would each have the care of their rooms and we did inspect and offer rewards. However each had a daily chore and a weekly chore as well. Daily chores would be clearing the table after meals, helping me prepare meals, cleaning up the great room, or the community bathrooms. The weekly chore was once a week we would deep clean common areas of the Lodge. You never knew when someone would drop in and want to tour the facility. I wanted to instill in these girls a pride of their surroundings. Many were not taught to take care of themselves and their surroundings. We taught table manners, and how to set the table, planning a meal and buying the groceries and preparing a meal. How to bake bread, soups, and their favorite things to eat. We poured ourselves into helping them grow up and be able to keep a home. Some come along with this training willingly and some did not. It was basically a "non-negotiable" part of living at Serenity Valley. The girls would help us mow the lawns, weed the flower beds and put in a garden. I am sure more than one girl was disgusted by my "manure tea" that I kept for watering the garden. We did harvest good tasting veggies.

    The garden spot was put in by a work team from Hot Springs; I was so excited to have a place to plant veggies. I love to dig in the dirt and watch God grow things in my garden. I often could be in there alone as the girls knew if I was going out there we would be weeding so they made themselves scarce when I was headed that way.

Chapter Three – Daily Life

Fall came to the Valley and school started for the girls. Stormharbor has a school on site at the boys Ranch. They taught each kid according to their abilities and each was given individual attention. Often kids would come in behind and would make up several grades while attending. I would take on the task of teaching music and choir that first year. I had been a piano teacher in Michigan for many years and loved teaching kids that they could make music. It was difficult however because we combined both boys and girls for that class so we had several incidents when I had to radio for assistance. We were given two way radios for use on the boys Ranch, they did not work at Serenity Valley. We were to call for assistance when there was an issue that required a firmer hand to resolve. I used it several times while teaching that year. I would call for assistance and the cavalry would come rushing into the classroom. Men from all over the Ranch and some ladies as well. This was to let the kids know that we never functioned alone and we were part of a bigger team. It is impressive to see for sure. Some kids would settle right down while others would ratchet up and need to be removed from the class room. It was never about fear, rather control and love.

The girls would often have homework, but a daily part of their lives was barn duty. Stormharbor had 13 horses that were used for riding and for Equine Therapy. Each house had barn chores, each house had a week when they were in the barn before school, feeding the horses and grooming them, after school the stalls were cleaned out and the barn was swept out. This was a challenge that I did not have to participate in Bill and the RI's would take the kids over and work beside them to get these chores accomplished. The houses would compete for trophies and there were score sheets on the wall of the barn so each kids could see how they were doing. Bill had never been around horses as a kid, I had. He did what any good city boy would do and got a book about horses to read, and did this before we left for Stormharbor. He came to me in utter bewilderment when he read that horses put out up to fifty pounds of manure a day. He was sure God would gift us with over achieving horses and he was not wrong. I am in awe of my husband for what he lived through with all those teenage girls and horses and the like.

We had a horse at Serenity Valley whose name was Chief. He was an old cutting horse and was donated to the ranch. After a horse barn was built at Serenity Valley we were given two horses and Chief was one. Every critter we had at Serenity Valley was female, and I know Bill was overwhelmed at times. He went down to the barn after the kids left for school one morning and was talking to Chief. That big old cutting horse walked over and wrapped his head and neck around Bill's as if to say it will be alright buddy, we are in this thing together. That is one of the reasons horses are used for therapy, they can sense and respond to the emotions we give them.

Bill will always be my hero for all that he had to overcome in order to be a great surrogate father to the girls. To this day many call him Dad and forever will be daughters to us.

Our house was to take many first place, second place and third place trophies during the years we were at Serenity Valley. The girls would be given them during chapel on Thursday nights. I loved seeing them light up with that trophy, they were also recognized for achievements at school and other activities. Often these were the first times that they had been given any awards. We made a big deal out of it for that very reason. Kids who fall through the cracks every day in school never know the feeling of wonder at having someone clap for them and hug them and encourage them for their accomplishments. We did that big time!

School years fall into a routine for us just like any other family. We had our fall activities and enjoyed the cooler temperatures. We tried to go places and see things they would not normally have the opportunity to do. We loved going to the Parks around our area. We found out that many of the kids who are abused never get to just be carefree and play. We were so surprised when the girls would rush over to the swings and slide and play like little kids. Their laughter was infectious, and they often complained when it was time to leave. We would frequent Petit Jean State park, Lake Nimrod State Park, Mount Magazine State Park, and many more. We often spent our own funds to take these trips as the Ranch would struggle often with funding. We believed that we were investing in the lives of these girls. This would eventually take a huge toll on our finances. God knew this too.

One thing that happened frequently at our house which I often instigated was pot holder wars. Now you ask yourself what I am talking about; Well, I could tell as the girls came through the door into the kitchen at night if they had had a good day or a terrible one. Each one would speak to me or they would occupy the stools at the serving counter and all talk at once telling me what had happened at school, barn or wherever they were. If they all came in sullen and quiet I knew that there was trouble brewing. I had in the previous months collected dozens of pot holders. Some had chicken heads on them and they flew more true and faster than the plain ones. They were in the drawers by my stove. I would wait until the first three girls passed by me and I would begin flinging them in all directions. Before you knew it the girls were throwing them back and laughing so hard they could hardly stand up. The tension was broken and all were at the serve through window talking all at once. God gave me that method of tension breaking and it worked over and over. Sometimes I got crazy and sprayed water and that usually turned into a water fight where we were all drenched. Laughter always followed and we got a clean kitchen floor in the process as well. God is so good to allow us the release valve of laughter when we believe that the whole world is against us.

We had school four days a week one day being reserved for seeing our wonderful Christian psychologist. She was a blessing in so many ways. We would be able to see how God was using her intervention in the lives of our girls through her time with them. She would make herself available to us as well. She was such a gift. Her faithful companion was Rascal her therapy dog. A very large Golden Retriever who loved each kid unconditionally.

Then came the weekends. Saturday was a day for sleeping in and having a big breakfast. I would let the girls decide what they wanted to eat. We had a huge gas range that Bill bought for Serenity Valley and it had a flat top griddle on it. We could cook several pounds of hash browns, eggs and bacon all at one time. We would make pancakes and heat up syrup, and chow down! Each one got her favorite. Sometimes I would even make waffles, or omelets, and they could choose the fillings. We had a wonderful time slowly working our way into the day. Teenagers can sleep most of their lives away, but if you have nightmares whenever you close your eyes you don't sleep well. We had many nightmare nights with the girls. Most of the terrible stuff that happened to them happened in the dark. We had night lights and hall lights and such to help quiet that fear. We were on call 24/7 if there was a need. It is just what you do when you love kids.

The next day was the Lord's Day and going to church was not optional with our house. We never forced the girls to believe what we believed. It was a good exercise in self-discipline for them to have to sit still and listen to the teaching, and of course there were boys there to watch when they got bored. I know that many girls loved going to church and we went out afterwards for lunch and some shopping as we were in a big city and the stores were handy. New girls had a one month probationary period where they had to be with a house parent or an RI when off Ranch. After the probation period we required that girls pair up when shopping. They were given a time limit to shop then we would meet them at the front of the store. We always told the girls that if there were to get caught shop lifting we would turn them in and have them face the consequences of their actions. Thank goodness we never had to do that. We did have a few that had a penchant to pick up things they could not pay for, and then have to take it back to where they picked it up from. We did give the girls an allowance and they had to decide to save or spend it. We gave council when asked, they did not often ask. We then had to confiscate all the candy and dole it out in a healthy manner.

Church and chapel were an important part of every week and we had chapel on Thursday nights. We sang and handed out barn awards or school awards. We often had guest speakers; they would bring a unique perspective to life for the girls. We had musicians, artists, poets, and preachers come and share. It was a time for the staff to get some encouragement from the Word of God and to soak in the fellowship of the others on the Ranch. The staff at Serenity Valley consisted of Bill and I and our RIs. So we often did not see the staff on the other ranch unless it was our day for staffing or we transported the girls back and forth from school. The isolation can work two ways, it can be good as you have more time to get your stuff done, or bad as you miss the support of the team aspect of this type of work. That was the draw-back to being seven miles away. If you needed help it would take up to 30 minutes for that help to reach you after they have been notified. In the future that would become a source of dissention between us and the "senior staff". We would see it play out many times in our time there. Logistically we were isolated. It was wonderful for the girls as they could be completely free outside and around the ranch as there were no boys or men beside Bill. They were relaxed and felt safe there. Mission accomplished in that respect! However when things got bad we needed the back up and were often left to find our way out of it by ourselves. We learned much at various trainings we would attend and were able to function better with this issue as time passed and we did not call for help as often.

One of the truly unique things that happened at the Ranch is that as time passed by we were adopted by different church groups and individuals. One such group that became a huge blessing to us and the kids was the ladies from the church "Community of Joy" in Hot Springs village. One afternoon we received a call from the office and were asked if a ladies group could tour our facility. Of course, I answered, and looked forward to sharing all that God was doing there with these ladies. We were to become good friends with the wonderful group of women. Their hearts were so big and the love they brought to the girls was pure and sweet. They started coming out for dinner once a month on Tuesdays. We named that event "Sundaes on Tuesday" because they brought ice cream and all the toppings for our dessert that night. We would have dinner together and then afterwards they would play games, work on homework, or just sit and talk to the girls. The girls came to love each and every lady who poured themselves in the lives of our girls. They provided Christmas presents for our kids, they raised money to buy two dishwashers, a fridge, and vacuum for the Lodge. They came and brought baked goods and taught the girls how to make bread. We looked forward to their times with us. They hosted a spaghetti dinner in our honor and we served the guests as they came in. Such a great outlet for the girls to learn to serve others who are serving you. How like our Savior to become the servant to servants. We were in the newspaper in Hot Springs village as we participated in the life of that community. The girls would go and rake leaves, wash windows and do other outside chores that needed doing for the seniors that were shut in there in the Village. Giving back to those who could no longer handle the physical labor needed to finish these tasks. Lots of laughter, but some complaining and whining as well. We are always teaching when these things come along, trying to get the kids to see beyond their feelings and help someone else. In doing this they are able to see that there are many who are less fortunate and this often helped them to be much happier at taking on these tasks for our community at large. Often Bill and an RI would make these trips as I was home keeping up with the myriad of paper work and one hundred other things that could not get done if the kids were home. We were to establish long term friendships through this place. The kids were able to feel the love of someone other than us, and to see Jesus Christ in the lives of those folks.

Stormharbor would often host youth groups from different churches who wanted to come and do a project with our kids. Fence painting, was a big one that needed doing! We had a group of young folks come to Serenity Valley and in two days completely fenced in our back pasture. One of our girls saw the opportunity to pit herself against some of those kids in a race to see who would finish first, she won. However everyone was completely obliterated when the project was done. The groups would stay and eat at Serenity Valley and we had a ball when that happened. Kids tell stories and joke around, they were just kids and it was wonderful when our kids would just blend in. So much of their lives they had been on the outside looking in on life. The other really cool thing about having outside groups was that the girls got to see how neat Christians could be. We would have chapels together and the singing was over the top wonderful. We had moments when you could close your eyes and picture heaven and all of us singing there. It made the dark times easier for me when that would happen.

Chapter Four – Taking Up Our Cross Daily

Fall was a wonderful time at the Ranch because it would finally cool off enough to have fun outside again. The kids would put up tents and sleep in the yard. We had a good time with that whole project because everyone is brave until the lights go out. It was not unusual to find the girls downstairs sleeping on the sofas and floor of the great room. They heard a noise and got scared and came in. I could never figure out why they just did not go to their rooms and their own beds. We would go to a park with a picnic lunch after church and eat and let the kids play. It seemed as if the earth had released a big sigh when the weather would cool down. Mind you for us from the Upper Peninsula it was fall for the whole winter. We grew to absolutely love the South and the whole beauty of the mountains, and serenity of the woods. The flowers and vegetation are so very different from the UP and so I had a whole new wonderful world open up to me to learn new plants and what I could grow.

We had just three girls through that first Christmas and then we began adding more girls. They would come from so many different back grounds. Yet all had a common denominator, they were wounded. We knew often before we would take a girl what had happened to her. However there were some that came and we found out after she was there for a while and began to trust us. I can only say that it never got any easier to hear the stories of hurt and pain, abandonment, abuse, betrayal. I would often have to leave the room and cry for a minute. Dry my tears and go back and hold them as they recited the horror and pain that had rained down on their lives. God knows I was never prepared for it and He also knew we would be the ones there to pick up the pieces, and lead them to the gentle arms of the Great Physician. I railed some nights when the nightmares would be really bad. Mostly I was angry at the evil one and what he had perpetrated on them. We had heard the statistics that one in three women/girls in the United States of America has suffered some type of sexual assault. That stat is staggering when you begin to process it. What has happened to our country? We have walked away from the Living God and placed our trust in the world. Doing that will insure that the evil one will hand you your head on a platter. He will consume our young people, leading them into destruction the likes of which you cannot even imagine. If you think we backed down you could not be more wrong. It just steeled my resolve to win them back for Christ. To show them the love and compassion of our Savior and Lord. The provide for them a place where they were safe and could take their time trusting until they could see Christ in us and the others on the Ranch who loved them before they knew them. We had one incident that rocked the house for a few weeks. We had a girl make a Ouija board and then sneak into the bathroom upstairs with a few other girls and start to ask it questions. Satan does not miss any opportunity to make his presence known and he stepped up there in a big way. One of our RI's found the girls and destroyed the board but not before she came face to face with a demon that had terrorized her as a teen. She called us and we responded and got the girls together in the great room of the lodge and began to talk about the power of the evil that can be unleased when given permission to enter into the lives and homes of those responsible.

    We had a long talk about the evil of that game and the results. We loved on them and we prayed with them, and sent them to bed. We then prayed around the Lodge asking for protection for us and the girls. It was dark and I stayed behind and slept in the great room that night. I was awakened by noises and sat up and looked around, I saw shadows moving from place to place in the kitchen, dining room and great room. I started to quote scriptures,

You are from God, little children, and have overcome them (evil spirits); because greater is He who is in you than he who is in the world! – 1 John 4:4

Then sang Jesus Loves Me about ten times, quoted some more scripture, the room lightened up and there was peace again in the house. We would do battle like that time and again. In my heart I knew that there was no place for fear in this battle and so I was at peace.

The battle is real and it is for keeps. We had many victories but we also saw kids go home and right back into the very things that would destroy them. We had a girl who before she left practiced some of her witch craft in the room at the head of the stairs. The other girls were frightened to pass the room. We called a group of believers from the other Ranch to come over and pray and read scriptures out loud taking back the room, and expunging it of the evil that was done there. The girls came home from school that day and ran upstairs, one came back down and said that the room was bright and she was no longer afraid. We did not tell her what we had done there, but were gratified that it was again a safe place for them to be.

The thief has come only to steal and kill and destroy; I have come that they may have life and have it abundantly, - John 10:10

We were standing in the gap for these girls and the evil one knew it. We had to work hard at staying well. We struggled with the depression that comes from being on the front lines and seeing so much destruction of human lives. We had to stay in the Word daily or else risk being weak when the time came to fight again.

I am sorry to say that often the biggest hurts came from other staff members. We expected it from the kids but not from the staff. We were supposed to be a team. We were not exempt from being hurtful to each other as well. When we first arrived we got one weekend off a month and part of one day a week. That is not much when you're so very tired the first day of your day off you were sick with exhaustion. Diarrhea, upset stomach, head ache, you name it you were obliterated. Day two was better, and Sunday we were back on duty by six in the evening. We found ourselves struggling to find time as a couple, to work through some of the stuff that arises naturally from being together and under stress. We had never worked together and now we were living and working together, along with two young women who were not our own. We were so blessed to have had some wonderful young women join the team at Serenity Valley. We did however have some difficult times, lots of tears and lots of laughter. Those stories are for another time. We are not perfect now and we were not perfect then. God gives much grace and we needed to give each other much grace. For the most part it worked well.

    I know you don't know me personally but those who do know that I love the Christmas season. I turn into a giant elf and can't wait to decorate the house and bake cookies and play Christmas music and wrap presents. I want everyone to be happy and all get along. I want there to be joy everywhere and much laughter. Well, "that aint a happenin"!!!!!! I was once again reminded that many of our kids did not have Currier and Ives Christmases. We were decorating the tree the first year and I had brought most of my ornaments over along with my angel tree topper. I encouraged the girls to help me decorate, for the most part all I got in response was negativity and whining! I could not imagine that they would not be excited to have Christmas. The Ranch had parties that were put on for the kids by local groups and churches. The presents under the tree numbered more than they had probably seen in all their lives. However their homes were not different and when they went home all that was there before would still be there. In fact we had some who could not go home for the holiday season. That was just awful for them and so they were negative and hard to live with. The emotions ranged from tears to all out anger. So my Christmas season morphed into something that I had never experienced before. I pushed ahead with my plans to bake cookies and to have a party at the Lodge for other houses to attend. We had the parties, opened the presents and pushed through the pain and hurt, and somehow January came along. Wow a new year.

That December Hannah came to the Ranch. She is one of the sweetest most loving young women you will ever meet. She has been a part of our family in the UP and was a great friend to our girls. She wanted to be a part of the ministry at Serenity Valley and so she became an RI. She was a God send for me as she knew me so well that she anticipated me. We spend hours in the kitchen together, grocery shopping, laughing, and working side by side. She loved the girls completely and they knew she was a friend. She could run and jump and keep up with them, she would become the big sister many never had. She would scold them and cajole them into doing their chores, and then play with them. We were to see a side of her that we had never seen before. She nurtured them and loved them. They were our family and by extension hers. We had other RI's and they each brought their own unique talents to the house. Camping and music, reading, and teaching. Each one was gifted in some way to bring a brightness to the lives of each girl. We were to find out much about ourselves as we worked with each RI. I am often "blunt" not meaning to hurt just to cut to the chase so to speak. I was taught the fine art of "southern gentility", graciousness, and patience. We encouraged each RI to find their way to reach the kids. We often had to reign in the riots that would happen when RI's found a new way to play. One in particular decided to ride the cookie sheets down the staircase and landed at the bottom just as the Director and guest came in the front door. Not missing a beat she smiled and went back upstairs to curtail the entourage that was waiting their turn. We had one RI who had a laugh that was identifiable from long distances away. It was infectious and we always ended up laughing with her.

She was a gift to the girls and to us. I am sure we did not spend enough time telling these young women what a gift they were. I hope if they read this they will know that we loved them all.

We were often gifted with chicken from a local company, they would donate thousands of pounds of chicken a year. So we became adept at cooking chicken. Every which way you can imagine. I loved to cook before the Ranch and wasted no time dragging out my favorite recipes and preparing them for the girls. One of Hannah's least favorite chores in the kitchen was deboning the chicken. She would rather do almost anything else but that. However we would cook chicken and debone it and freeze the meat and make chicken broth with the rest. She became rather efficient as time went by. We would introduce the girls to cuisine from many parts of the world. I loved to cook new and exciting things and they would balk at first but generally would come around. I had some of my own tried and true recipes to fall back on when the day was too crazy to spend much time preparing dinner. At the height of our time there we were feeding twelve for breakfast and dinner. The kids ate lunch at the other ranch. I know that I would search recipes for something that would appeal to them all but rarely did everyone rave about what was served. I was determined to serve well balanced meals and the vegetables were always an important part of the menu plans. We would then take those menus and prepare grocery lists from them. We had to keep count of all that was served and make a report that would then track commodities. That was just one of the ways we were able to stretch our food budget. There were many times when we would fix something the kids asked for and one of their favorites was build your own pizza night. The possibilities were limitless and we had fun seeing what each one could accomplish with the ingredients provided. We even made our own pizza dough and they had to stretch it to make their creations. We always had left overs so Sunday night became our left over night and we invited anyone who did not want to cook to come and eat with us. To this day I am to trying to figure out how to cook for just two of us! I know that one of the most important thing to some of our kids was that there was food available.

One girl would ask me every day what we were having for dinner that night. It became a ritual between she and I and I understood it was a source of security for her to know that she would have enough to eat. Others would come to us and hoard food. We would find food in their rooms and it would then get moldy and bad. I would sit them down and rather than scolding them for taking the food, offer them granola bars and snack crackers to have in their rooms. The proviso was that they were not to leave open food in their drawers and on the floor under their beds. That relieved them of the fear of going to bed hungry. We had a Labrador named Ebony, and a Scottie called Keely, they would sniff out the crumbs so in the end all was well. Food however would come into play over and over with different girls. The poorer the family the greater the fear. We had to convince them not to circle their plates with their arms and hang over them, no one would take their food away, not ever while they were at Serenity Valley.

I like to celebrate each birthday in a really big way. We would make a cake of their choosing and have ice cream and invite the Ranch family to come and have a big party to celebrate. We had decorations and the girls could choose what they wanted to see. We would put up streamers and buy presents. The other girls often made presents from the stuff they had in their possession at the time. It was a time of joy and sadness as many had never had a party of their own before that time. Girls being girls though we managed to laugh and have pictures taken and just enjoy the whole process.

The girls were always ready to have a party if it meant having the boy's houses there. We were able to make opportunities for them to learn proper ways to socialize. We did not have any illusions about mixing teenage girls and boys. They are hormone driven, and so we kept a close eye. Mr. Bill was always vigilant about keeping his girls close by. We were not always successful but we tried. After all there were six to eight of them and three or four of us. Keeping a relaxed mental attitude was crucial however not always possible. To say we never lost our tempers or got frustrated would be a lie, and that was one of the best things about having a team approach, we could step away from the house and cool down before things blew up.

That sounds good in theory but it did not always work that way. We are human beings and can be pushed to our outer limits and beyond. We love them but they did not trust us. It would take a long time before that would kick in so invariably we would have confrontations. Often I would be confronted by an angry hurt girl and she would be verbally abusive and aggressive in her behavior. I would have to stand my ground quietly and listen to her and give her time to cool down. Bill did not like the way they were treating me and he would want to come to my defense. We worked out a signal that I would use to let him know if I needed him to intervene. He often was the one practicing the ministry of presence. He could not go upstairs in the Lodge and I could, he could not and would not touch the girls, I could. We worked out giving side hugs and that was monitored so that no touch could be misconstrued by them as sexual in any manner. I was so glad our own daughters were there on Ranch and would come and spend time at the Lodge. The girls could see a good relationship between father and daughters by watching their interactions. We were so blessed to have them there to come and help out.

We would have an event about once a month known as a "Coming to Jesus". We would be having trouble between the girls and something would trigger a big eruption. We would bring the girls all downstairs and sit them around the dining room and the great room where they could see each other but not talk to each other. We always knew most of what had happened, but as we talked to each girl in the office we would then learn about so much more that we did not know. Contraband that had come into the house. Cigarettes, and stuff they knew we would not allow. We would listen to them tell their stories and in the end we were able to clean up the house. If however we believed there was something in their rooms that they were not allowed to have and they did not fess up we would have to "toss the room". That became the RI's responsibility. They got very good at searching in places the girls were sure we would never look. Floor boards in the attic, in the toilet tanks, in the linen closets, taped to the bottom of their drawers, in their socks, and luggage. You name it they found it. We then had consequences. Yep they had to do some extra chores. One of my very favorites was picking up Magnolia pods in the front yard. We had an enormous Magnolia tree and the pods were huge and would become projectiles when the lawn was mowed. They had to be picked up. These projects were done alone except of course for me checking on them. That often gave me time to talk just to them and love on them and build up our relationship a bit. I would like to say that we did not have many of those "Coming to Jesus" parties but that would not be true.

Sitting on the front porch was another way we could talk to each other without the stress of looking at each other. The stories that I heard while rocking on the front porch will be embedded in my mind forever. First loves, biggest disappointments, anger, betrayal, regrets... and much more. These topics were freely discussed because we were safe. We were rocking and looking at the beauty of the Ranch and everyone was safe. You see safety was the most important thing they needed in order to begin to heal. They were not always on alert, they could relax and play and talk, and heal. I loved the porch, I have always been a porch sitter and knew the joy of being gently rocked and loved on. We had flower boxes full of flowers and pots of every size and shape all across the porch. I had wind chimes that we had bought and the dulcet tones would sooth and calm. I loved those times because I would talk about Jesus, His love, His grace and mercy. How he was right there for the girls if they would just seek Him. We would tell stories and laugh, and tell jokes. I would hear about lost loves and new ones. I would hear about school issues and the cutest boys ever. They were safe and secure, and loved. That is all I wanted for them, to have a safe beautiful place to heal. They would bring all their hurt and pain with them into the valley, and the evil one would come along too. We were the first line of defense for them and would stand in that gap for as long as it took for them to finally begin to trust and heal. We had no illusions that all would welcome what we had to offer. I am sure that I was called many names not fit for print, and I can assure you that some hurt me deeply. I am the type of person who is all in when it comes to serving the Lord. I know that He suffered so much greater pain than I ever did there. I also know that He loves those girls and He loves me. That is the great equalizer in all that was said and done during our years at Serenity Valley.

And He was saying to them all, "If anyone wishes to come after Me, he must deny himself, and take up his cross daily and follow Me." - Luke 9:23

Taking up your cross daily is a difficult thing to master. However when you do, you realize that at the end of the road Jesus Christ will carry your cross for you when you no longer have the strength to pick it up. We had many days when the alarm clock went off, and as we crossed the grass to start the day at the Lodge, we prayed as we walked, for the strength and patience, and love to be there for the girls. We were never disappointed, God showed up and blessed the day in ways too numerous to count. We had extra strength and patience and grace and mercy given to us over flowing. I am in awe of our Savior Jesus Christ for His provision.

...and he who does not take up his cross and follow Me is not worthy of Me. He who has found his life will lose it and he who has lost his life for My sake will find it. - Matthew 10:38-39

To know that what you are able to do has eternal value, trumps all the hurt and pain of service. God will use these days for our good and for His glory. In the years since, we have looked back and thought about the time we were there. We have sifted through the good and peeled away the bad until all that is left is our obedience and our commitment to those girls.

We loved them all, there were a few it was hard to like some times but we loved them all. To this day we have relationships with many of them. What a blessing! Working with at risk teenagers of any gender adds an element of determination to those relationships. We know based on our years working in the prisons that the end result of bad decisions often driven by hurt and betrayal is incarceration. We were keenly aware that that was always a possibility. We were driven to pray harder and work harder so that they would see that they have value not only to us but to our Heavenly Father. Earthly fathers often ruin their relationships with their daughters, and so it is all that much harder to teach them to believe that they have a Heavenly Father that desperately wants a relationship with them for time and eternity. That is a process that the Holy Spirit plays a key role in. Waiting for teaching moments when their hearts are soft to hear about what was accomplished on the cross on their behalf. We watched carefully for those moments to come and prayed we would recognize them and take advantage of them when they did.

Chapter Five – Listen, Listen, Love, Love

We welcomed visits from folks from home as they would come and visit and bring their own brand of fun with them. We had two visits from the Lung family. Jill and I were very good friends back in Michigan and I welcomed them with open arms. Darrin came ready to help Bill do work projects that required two sets of hands. There was a ton of laughter and some really good eating. We had a make your own pizza night and it was a huge hit for the kids. We also welcomed Greg and Elizabeth Peterson Family from Gladstone Michigan. They brought Spencer and Danny and Bethany. We had so much fun with them as well and Bethany made connections with the girls and began friendships that she would carry through in the years to follow. Again these families were a part of our bigger church family at Grace Church in Gladstone, and we had been friends for many years. We also welcomed the Cass family Julie and her husband, his friend and their sons who came and rewired the whole panel at the Lodge and a paid for the materials needed to complete that huge job.

One of the ways that the Ranch had of keeping costs down was a wonderful building known as donations. We were up the mountain from Hot Springs Village, one of the biggest retirement communities in Arkansas. We were supported by churches in the Village and we were given household items, clothes, and kitchen items as well as anything else we would pick up and bring back up the mountain. We were so very blessed by that relationship! The girls absolutely loved going to donations. It was a treat to be able to go and look through all the things that came up the mountain that day. We found appliances for the kitchen, and pictures for the walls, bedding and clothes. We just had a ball and it was difficult to keep the number of things that the kids wanted to a reasonable number.

We finally had to make a rule that they had to bring back the same amount that they took so that their rooms would not begin to sag from the sheer volume of things that they took. For kids who have had little in their lives to call their own it was a virtual paradise of wonderment. I knew I could take them to donations and count on a few hours of unbridled joy as they shopped for free.

We got any number of great things there and were always amazed at what would come up with the next truck load. I don't think it had the same attraction for the boys as it did for our girls, I had a ball in there myself and was able to furnish much of the Lodge with items we were given from big hearted and loving folks from all over but mostly from the Village. This was just another way that the Body of Christ showed their love for the kids at Stormharbor. We would also have volunteer groups come and mow lawns and fix bikes and cars and trucks. They would build and repair buildings as needed, they would take the time to talk to the kids and share a bit of themselves with them. The kids came to care for many of them, as their volunteerism stretched out over many years. They became as much a part of the ranch as the regular staff, and well loved. Each one brought a unique perspective on life and their wisdom. We enjoyed just sitting and talking to them and hearing their stories. There were war veterans, school teachers, business men and women, and just about every walk of life you can mention. Such a rich heritage they imparted to the kids. Quite often their children and grandchildren were far away so they adopted our kids as their own. This was such a neat thing to watch as each would find something with which to connect to our kids with. God's people stepped into the gap in these young lives and made a difference just by showing up and loving them.

This was a unique and wonderful example of the Body of Christ here on earth ministering to the wounded and lonely and needy. God set this in motion and we were the recipients of the blessings that ensued. I am humbled to this day at the sacrifices made on behalf of the ranch and our kids.

Coming to Stormharbor and Serenity Valley was an education in ranching that I had not expected to have. You see Stormharbor had at that time about thirteen horses and over fifty head of cattle. They used the cattle to keep the Equine Program afloat. So needless to say we got to experience a "Round-Up"! The cattle had to be gathered up and given injections and checked over each spring. We had the babies and the mama's to separate and return to separate pastures. The boys really got into the cowboy thing, while I think most of the girls were content to stay out of the way. The herding aspect of the process could be quite dangerous. The cows were normally quite calm and pleasant but when they are herded by four wheelers and guys on horses they become frightened and tend to bolt. They are huge animals and so we took every opportunity to stay on the fence and out of the way. I worked with Candy to prepare the injections and let Bobby and the guys give them. It would take most of an afternoon before all was said and done. Everyone was dirty and hot and tired, and the cows were again in the pasture placidly eating and ignoring us. Whew! Couldn't wait to get home and clean up and eat.

Equine Therapy was just getting started when we arrived at the Ranch. Several staff members had attended the training and were back on Ranch ready to get the whole thing up and running. I saw amazing things when they would work with the kids and horse together. The horses are so intuitive and responsive to the kids and their moods. They would do training with the staff and we could see the way the horses would respond to hurt and pain, anger and aloofness. They would give as good as they got when the kids were angry the horses would walk away, or stay away from them even when given commands. The kids were able to see how others respond to their emotions and how the horses would be happy and responsive when the kids were happy and responsive. It truly is a God given window into the souls of these wounded kids. The kids developed relationships with various horses and wanted to ride them when there was trail riding, or working out in the ring. I saw timid girls blossom when they were given a horse to love and take care of. Conversely they would see the animal walk away or run away when they approached it with anger and aggression. We monitored the girls closely to make sure they did not hurt the horses. We know that often kids who have been abused will act out their pain on animals. We could not always prevent it but when we knew that it was happening we kept the animals at a safe distance from them. We had a beautiful black lab, and she would sit and take the abuse. I never wanted that to happen and there were serious consequences when it did. Kids needed to learn to process their pain in such a way as to not hurt themselves or others around them. Cutting was often a result of this pain turned inward. Kids would tell us that it relieves their pain to cut themselves. Again this is an outward symptom of a tremendous pain. We knew that until they would start to process what had happened and work through it, we would see these types of things crop up. I learned through really good training not to respond in an emotional way to any of these behaviors no matter how upset they made me. I would choose to step away from the house and calm down then come back and respond to the behavior with practical solutions. We would give each girl a journal to write in and tell them that it was their safe place to put their thoughts. We would send them upstairs to write when their anger turned into rage at seemingly insignificant events. They had every right to be mad and even to rage however we needed to teach them where and when to release those emotions. We put a punching bag in a tree and would put boxing gloves on them and let them punch the bag until they were exhausted. This would release the emotions in a healthy way and tire them out enough to be able to have a conversation about what was happening. There was a four word motto at our house that we learned in prison. "Listen, listen, love, love." This would open doors for us as time went by to be able to hear the stories about the pain and sorrow, and to let them grieve what was lost due to the abuses they suffered. It was rare but there were some girls who never opened up to us. We just prayed they would open up to Mrs. Linda, or others of the staff who might be able to lead them to Christ, who ultimately was the only one who could heal their broken hearts and shattered spirits. Physical activity was a great outlet for the emotions that built up inside them.

We would send them out to the basketball court to shoot hoops, send them running around the Ranch, or up and down the hill in the back pasture. We would see the pain ease on their faces and eventually they were calm again and life continued on.

I realized what an awesome privilege it was for the girls to come to trust us and to share their lives with us. I am humbled to this day by the number of them that are still in contact with us. I have had calls to talk and to cry, to ask for recipes, and to share joys. We have received baby pictures and wedding announcements. They know that they are loved to this day by us and the young ladies who were our RIs. We know that God took us there for His purposes and we are blessed to have been surrogate parents for a time for the girls. That love and trust was hard fought and won. We are still processing the time we spent there both good and bad. The results are up to the Almighty and we will have the final picture when we all get to heaven.

Just when everything is going along fine the evil one once again shows up at Serenity Valley. I had placed crosses on the walls in each of the girls' rooms. One in particular was given to us by the wife of one of the board of directors. It was a beautiful mosaic cross and very heavy. We had mounted it carefully as we knew it would get damaged if it fell down, or could hurt someone. We received a call to interview for a new placement, went to the interview and prayed about taking this young woman. Her family had been practicing witchcraft and her traditions were steeped in it. We decided to take her in and the very first day we put her in the room with the mosaic cross it fell off the wall. I was stunned that it had fallen and so put it back even sturdier than before. That cross would fall off that wall for days. I began to sense that the evil one had a purpose in this event and was challenging us. I was witnessing to this young woman and telling of her of Jesus's love for her and the sacrifice He made for her at Calvary. I would walk into that room and pray out loud and sing praise and worship songs. One day about a month after she came to live at Serenity Valley she asked me if I would tell her how to become a believer, I sat on the side of her bed under that cross and led her down the Roman Road to salvation in our Lord Jesus Christ. That cross never fell off that wall again during our time at Serenity Valley. We would see this phenomenon repeated in other ways throughout our time at Serenity Valley. I can honestly say that as time went by my reaction became one of calm confidence and peace. I know Jesus Christ purchased my salvation at the cross of Calvary and so I am empowered. I will not sit and take any guff from evil as it has been soundly defeated and the evil one knows that truth himself. Girls were being redeemed from the evil one to a life in Christ that would prove to be a bigger testimony of His love and mercy and grace, than any spoken word. Glory to God for His faithfulness to stand in the gap and provide for us eternal life and a life filled with joy and purpose here on earth. It is a message that our kids were not familiar with in many of their lives, yet it was the truth and has the power to free them and did!

Chapter Six – Jesus Was With Him

We had passed the one year mark in August 2007. Summers on Ranch were crazy busy and the house parents were exhausted by the time school would start again in the fall. However August of 2007 would become for all of us a watershed time because of an event that happened at the end of that month.

We had an older couple on Ranch who were dearly loved. Maggie and Mike had retired to the Ranch to live out their years and serve the kids. Maggie taught so many boys and girls to read we lost count. Mike opened a wood shop and taught the boys for years how to use tools and make new or repair broken items. They were soft spoken, Godly folks. They were walking testimonies to God's love and faithfulness. Mike had started exhibiting mild symptoms of forgetfulness and we were getting concerned for his safety. We all had two way radios and so we agreed in a staff meeting that we would keep watch on him throughout the day and check in. He would take a walk every morning up the road and out the pasture and back. Jackie and Steven lived near there so we had folks around and they kept an eye out for him.

One morning Mike took off for his walk and Maggie did not see him go. He left behind his glasses, his wallet, and his coat. It was August and the heat index was in the 100s at the height of the day. I am not sure who got on the radio first but the call went out asking if anyone had seen Mike out walking. When we did not hear back folks began looking around the Ranch to see if he could be found. He did not turn up in any of the regular places so then we started to get more aggressive in looking. The guys got on the four wheelers and began looking down the Ranch road toward the highway, in the far pastures and up behind the boys houses in the hills. Hours went by and still no sign of him. Where could he have gone? We began to speculate that someone may have picked him up and that he could not remember who he was or where he lived. Or perhaps he had wandered into the hills and fallen and could not call for help. We also started to pray and begin to ask for help off Ranch. People responded in a way that I had never seen in my life. We had folks from the community at large come with their four wheelers, they searched on foot following a grid pattern. We had search and rescue teams with dogs, both rescue dogs and cadaver dogs. The "Air National Guard" planes began flying around and the forest service stepped up their assistance. The kids were seeing all this happening and it impressed on them the seriousness of John's disappearance and what it may cost if we did not find him. During this whole time Maggie was helping out wherever she could. She was calm and quiet. At the height of this whole event we had people signing in and searching and coming in for water and food. The Ranch provided a place for them to sleep and fed them. The kitchen was constantly fixing meals or cleaning up. I went over to help and took the girls with me. They cleaned up the tables and helped clean up the chapel. We were told that we were out of ice, and fruit, and lunch meat, and other things that we had used up to feed the searchers. So a prayer meeting was called in the dining hall and I pulled the girls into it. We asked God to meet the needs of this long list we had. Almost before we had said amen, a man stuck his head in the door and asked if we could help him unload his pickup truck. Inside that truck bed were the very things we had asked God for just minutes before. Its impact on us and the girls was so very powerful. God always shows up just on time! That happened over and over with churches and groups who had heard about the search on TV and radio. We were the recipients of God's grace through God's people.

  This search went on for more than a week and there were no clues. Teams who had a record of always finding the lost were disappointed and their dogs were exhausted and beat up. They would come in and lay the dogs down in the classroom and bathe their paws and bandage them and let them sleep in the quiet air conditioned rooms. They were so very weary and discouraged. They had to sign in and out so that their safety was assured and we did not lose anyone that was out there. Maggie would comfort them by saying "Either Mike is with Jesus, or Jesus is with Mike." Whichever way, it was alright with her. We were given numerous opportunities to witness to folks who came to help. Another really cool story from that event was this; Mike's favorite hymn was "Trust and Obey", and so as the many teams on foot were searching they were singing this hymn over and over. It echoed through the hills and valleys of the mountain ranges as they walked and searched. Many of the boys would join in the foot search. They were impacted by the lives and love of Mike and Maggie. Finally it was over a week and the Labor Day holiday had passed and many had to go back to their lives. The search was tearfully called off the Tuesday after Labor Day. We had searched for miles and miles, called hospitals and shelters, and we continued to do that for a long time afterward. Jackie had been on strong pain killers and she would tell you that she saw Mike in a tree at the end of the pasture road by their house. Jackie went home to be with the Lord that fall and we mourned her passing.

      As time went on the search continued. There was never any sign of Mike found. Vultures were occasionally seen circling and the men would take four wheelers to check it out. We thought that once the leaves were down in the Autumn something would turn up. Maggie waited patiently but there was never any sign of Mike found. We officially celebrated Mike's life two years later. I know in my heart of hearts that when they are both in heaven that reunion will be so very sweet and we will finally have the answers about what happened to Mike on that day he walked out of our lives. The kids were impacted by that event in ways that will continue throughout their whole lives. "Trust and obey for there's no other way, to be happy in Jesus but to trust and obey," those words are indelibly imprinted on their souls. The answers to prayer, the tears and frustrations, and finally the acceptance that brought peace.

Chapter Seven – Wrapped in the Lord

Later that fall Mrs. Jackie went home to be with the Lord. We celebrated her life. She was a fantastic vocalist and had made a CD of her music. Scooter decided he would approach a Christian radio station in Nashville to see if he could sell her CDs and donate the funds to help run the Ranch. The morning he was to leave for Nashville his and Jackie's house caught fire and burned down. He lost most everything they had together. There is a sweet picture of Scooter consoling the kids as they watch the fire. This man was truly a Godly man and instead of folding up from all the hurt and pain he went to Nashville and talked to that announcer on the station. They did sell some of Mrs. Jackie's music. A few weeks after that happened Scooter was using a saw and slipped, running his hand into the blades. They rushed him to Conway to try and save his fingers. They were able to sew them back on but one is still damaged. All the while the kids are watching to see if he would walk away from his faith. He never did. He is an amazing man. I was honored to know him and to serve with him there. I believe Scooter was sifted and found faithful. We all were sifted in many ways as we served Christ in those valleys. God would test and bless in so many ways as the weeks became years.

We saw staff come and go. Burn out is very high in the full time childcare business. The administration needed to find a way to give the staff enough down time to recover. We were given amazing training on many areas of abuse and psychological disorders. We were exposed to some of the foremost Christian teachers in this area and we were never disappointed when we were sent to seminars. We eventually used everything we learned in one way or another. However when you have been on the front lines for a long time your weapons begin to get to heavy to lift. I have said time and again, Christianity is the only place where they shoot their wounded.

We had houseparent's who loved what they were doing and dedicated themselves and their finances, and they were all in. When they got depleted instead of a sabbatical, they were dismissed and new ones were brought in to the detriment of the kids in their houses who had formed deep relationships with those folks. Much about full time childcare needs to be evaluated from the perspective of the folks who are on the front lines. They need to be listened to, and heard, and changes made on that basis. We were surrounded by intelligent and thoughtful folks whose only bias was for a better life for the kids we took in. It is shameful to waste the resource of a great set of houseparent's because they were pushed to their limits and burned out.

We had a few other bumps in the road during that late summer and early fall time. I woke up one morning to a pain that took my breath away. It was insistent and nothing would make it stop. I stayed home that day and after the kids left for school Bill came home to check on me. I was crying in earnest and knew something was terribly wrong. Bill took me to the emergency room and they found a kidney stone had lodged in the duct. I was given a shot for pain and an IV and a room to begin the odyssey of passing a kidney stone. It took all night and it passed. I slept most of that time as we were beyond exhausted. I was discharged a new women (so to speak) and two weeks later had that same pain and went through the whole thing all over again. It is not something you would wish on your worst enemy! God was there and again it passed. I have stones still in both kidneys but learned that dehydration was a key component in the process. So I bought myself a quart jar with a handle and filled it three times each day and drank it down. We were Yankees and had never dealt with the high heats that drain the body of its fluids and make you sick. We learned the hard way, but we did learn. We went for years without health insurance and so it was understood that we would need to be very sick before we would spend the money on health care. We were already in our fifties and the pace of life there was taxing even to the ones who were most fit. We saw the grace of God over and over in taking care of our needs. However we probably should have gotten medical care more than we did as we are paying today for the things we put off then. We also know that we are living in bodies of corruption and that someday as preordained, our bodies will go back into the ground and become dust. I am okay with that process and so don't spend much time contemplating my mortality. God is in charge of the day and hour and manner of my death, so I will just keep on with life!

We would find the provision of the Lord for us in so many unexpected ways. Paying cash for medical care helped us to keep the balances lower. We finally were able to apply for a health insurance through the state of Arkansas. We were able to see the dentist through this plan as well. We were well into our fifties and feeling the long hours and physical toll of the lifestyle we were living. Many nights we were in pain but God was faithful to keep us and give us the strength to get up the next morning and provide all that the girls needed. It was truly walking by faith and not by sight. Try it and see how the Lord provides your needs in ways so unexpected and wonderful. We were receiving some support from our friends back in Michigan and from Grace Church, our home church. It would always come just in time to cover our needs. It built us up and helped us to know that they were back home praying for us and supporting us. We were a team with them in this venture. They were there for us to call home and pray with, to have them come and visit, to get unexpected cards and letters. Even money came in from them at just the right time.

This speaks to the importance of teaming up with your missionaries both stateside and out of country. We were learning lessons about God's provision daily through the love and faithfulness of our fellow believers. We later applied this as our own kids left the states to become missionaries in

Albania. The "just in time" nature of a card or letter, the call and prayer time was such a food for our souls and spirits. It is critical that we view ministry as a team sport. We are not solitary soldiers in this battle for souls, and if we think we can go it alone we are easy picking for the evil one.

Time seemed to fly by on the Ranch as we took more girls and became more comfortable with the workings of the Ranch. We had some great family times at Serenity Valley. We had Anita paint a saying on the wall over the serve-through there which said this: "Having someplace to go is home, having someone to love is family, having them both is a blessing!"

We knew that many of our girls came from difficult homes. We also knew that we would only be able to be a part of their lives if they allowed it to happen. I decided early on in this whole process that I was going to make the type of home environment for them that I created for my biological girls. One of my all-time favorite things to do is to pop popcorn and watch a movie. We would haggle about which movie we were going to watch and then I would go to the kitchen and start the popcorn. None of that stuff from a box for me! I popped it in a pan and added butter and let them put salt or other toppings on as they wanted to. We had added enough chairs and couches to the Great Room that we could comfortably seat more than fifteen. The kids got their bowls and water and spread out to enjoy the feature. We probably saw the movie "Honey" a million times. I am just kidding however we came to know the music and the girls could quote it line for line. I eventually took it out of circulation for the mental health of the staff. We were given lots of videos, and Bill and I purchased more than fifty movies ourselves, it was a form of self-preservation! During the movies Bill would often fall asleep, he would say he was just resting his eyes. We were fine with that. Often there was discussion about what could and could not be a topping for popcorn and the newest one for me was sugar. I put a stop to that as they would just get more animated as the evening went on when I wanted the opposite effect. We all know that if mama ain't happy ain't nobody happy so the girls would relent when I put my foot down. We gave in on other more negotiable items as the situation warranted. Compromise is a wonderful principle for them to learn.

We would also spend time working in the flower beds together and planting the flower boxes and weeding all these things. It was a big project and most of the time I would hear grumbling at the beginning but then some would realize they liked the beauty surrounding them and would take ownership when they produced beautiful blooms.

We loved playing cards and board games and would have fun with these things as well. For the most part we did our best to incorporate family times and insisted that everyone participate even those who did not want to at first eventually joined in on the fun. There was much laughter and great memories for the girls.

When the hottest months arrived our second year Bill had a brilliant idea. Instead of always running to the lake to cool off he bought three of the biggest tarps he could find. He then placed them down the hill next to the Lodge and created a "slip and slide". You would have thought we spent a million dollars for all the laughter and fun they had with those tarps. We did go through a great deal of the cheapest dish soap, as it was much faster if it was soaped down. It was worth it to hear the laughter and see the fun the kids had with that invention. Girls would relax and have fun when there were no boys around. Just being a kid was of paramount importance to them at that time. There would be time enough to make all those adult decisions. We battled to keep the environment as light hearted as possible. When you have a house full of teenage girls you will always have "DRAMA!" We did and often it would come in spurts. It was the domino effect when one was having a bad day others would decide that it was time to air whatever grievance they had with each other at the same time. I often felt like a referee in a verbal boxing match. I would have to talk to the teachers and see what happened at school. Often they would call the house parents and tell what had transpired that day, so we had the heads up before the kids arrived back at the Ranch. Sometimes we did not get called and we would have our hands full. We would not tolerate any physical violence no matter what had been said! I knew that if we opened that Pandora's Box we would have a full blown war on our hands. I could tell we were close and so we would get dinner behind us and have a "coming to Jesus" party to see if we could find our way back to calm. Many times it was through prayer and listening we would find the answers to these eruptions. Discernment comes from listening to the leading of the Holy Spirit.

We would sometimes ask for help from the senior staff in order to get a resolution before bed time. We found throughout the years that the worst violence and abuse had often happened after dark to these girls. We could see a pattern develop in which there was trouble at night. As we got wiser in caring for them we could spot the pattern with a girl and knew she was having nightmares or flashbacks. It is inconceivable to me as a mother that any parent could hurt their child, and to this day it grieves me to hear the stories of abuse that so many have suffered. We would leave hall lights on and closet lights and I had night lights as well. Just the comfort from those would often aide in sleep for some. If not, I would sit in their room, rub backs, sing, pray out loud or just be present until they slept. I did not want them to be on sleeping pills however we would go through quite a bit of melatonin during these days of trouble. We, as a staff, would often take a new placement that was taking many high powered drugs to curb behaviors. Our thinking was, we would have to begin, with medical help, to wean them off them in order to see who these kids really were. We were monitored closely by medical doctors as we began this process, and found that a great deal of the time the kids were completely different when they were not medicated into passivity. Yes there were times when they were given medications for help with diagnosed issues, however when we finally got most of them down from these medications they were quite different kids. Each was crying out for love and help in their own way. Often they had found that causing trouble would garner them the attention that they were not getting any other way. Many were extremely bright and funny kids who just needed a forum to grow and develop their personalities, gifts and talents.

Along the way on this adventure I began to realize some personal truths, first about my faith and then about myself. I realized that I truly loved being a care taker. I've worn many hats in my lifetime and this one was one of my favorite. No, this ministry is not for everyone and I know that deep in my gut. It will open up all your old wounds and expose them to the light. It will force you to take long hard looks at your tightly held belief systems. It will challenge your marriage, your health, your relationships and you're very core.

We would see personality traits that we possessed and knew that they needed to be addressed and the Holy Spirit was at work in my life during my time at Serenity Valley. I will develop that later but suffice to say that we were never the same after this time in our lives. The kids could push you and step on your last nerve with high heels and you would find that you did not have such a good hold on your temper. You would find that they would challenge you on a Biblical doctrine and you were back in the Word of God digging to once again center yourself on the truths of your faith. Dealing with witchcraft, sexual abuse, physical abuse, and emotional trauma would force me over and over to go back and examine what I knew to be true and what the evil one was dishing out that day as lies cloaked in truth. I thought I was prepared for front line battle but it soon became obvious that I had much to learn and was doing so while in battle. I cannot emphasize enough how prepared you need to be when you are walking onto the front lines of battle with the evil one. He does not fight fair and will use every weapon at his disposal to reclaim the lives and hearts and souls of the kids we were fighting so hard to keep safe long enough to see the truth of a life in Christ.

Bill likes an illustration that we heard one time which goes as follows; the Titanic has sunk and the water is brutally cold. You have a life boat and you are rowing around pulling folks out of the water in order to save their lives. The sun comes up and as it does half of them jump back into the water losing their lives right before your eyes! We experienced that phenomenon over and over. You see for many, the life that they were living was the only one they had ever known and so when you presented freedom from it through Christ, they would accept and then get scared and go backwards. We had so many kids who loved the very folks who were abusing them, and they wanted a relationship with these people that would give them the security that kids crave, however over and over they would go home on visits and come back more angry and hurt than before they left. Because the environment that they were in had not changed and they could finally see that it was a sick environment. That did not negate the love that they had for their folks. In fact many kids vow to go home and help their folks to get better. However that is rarely the case. It still is a source of great pain for the kids as they want their families to be well, most will not see that in their lifetime. Without intervention they will go on to create households that contain the same sickness and abuse that they grew up in. God is the great equalizer in this equation. We know and witnessed divine intervention and saw great miracles of healing along the way. We had hoped to create an environment in which there was freedom and safety for that process to begin in their lives. In fact it did and it also germinated healing and changes in our own lives. For that we continue to give God all the glory for what He has done through this whole experience.

The thief comes to steal, and kill, and destroy, but I have come that they may have life and have it abundantly. - John 10:10

We were to become intimately acquainted with the many names of the evil one, the thief being just one of the many ones he would have. We watched him rob the girls of their peace and security and their self-worth. We watched our loving Lord and Savior heal those wounds and build a loving relationship that would last a lifetime. What an amazing God we serve.

      We developed a tradition as each new girl arrived we would gently welcome them to Serenity Valley. That first night there was always a traumatic event for each one. We had been gifted with the most beautiful quilts created by a group of church ladies in Hot Springs Village. They made each one unique and the colors and patterns and pictures were so creative and wonderful. We would lay them all out along the dining room table and allow each new girl to choose one for themselves. It was a gift and each took theirs home when they left us. We would watch as they would touch each one and begin to be amazed that someone they did not know would create this just for them. For many it was their first time receiving a gift of such great beauty. Once the quilt was chosen we would take their picture with them wrapped in it. What a precious picture of how our Lord and Savior Jesus Christ purchased us and wrapped us in His love and He did that even before we knew Him! Later that week I would take their picture and frame it and put it up on the wall in the dining room. That was our wall with family photos, and theirs belonged there for as long as we were taking care of them. Many of the girls had never had a picture taken and put up on the wall and they were excited to see the finished product. I will never forget the many faces that we placed on that wall. Each and every girl had an impact on my life in some way. Each one brought with them hopes and dreams, laughter and tears, hurt and pain. Each brought to us the possibilities that come with hope in the Lord. We prayed and prayed for each of them and continue to do so to this very day. I know that God is not finished with them yet, and for those who have strayed away from Him we pray for a great and loving family reunion. We have been privy to many events in their lives through social media. We are Mom and Dad to many girls and some guys. We are so humbled and blessed to have been given the precious gift of time in their lives to pour ourselves into them and allow them to impact us.

Many would come to the Ranch with just a few items in a plastic bag. Others would have many suitcases of nice things. We would have to go through each and every item and weed them out and place some in storage for their eventual return home. We had a dress code for school which was jeans and a Stormharbor shirt. That was the great equalizer for the kids who had nothing with those who had much. I would eventually start a storage closet which held jeans in every size, under wear, socks, shoes, night clothes, shirts and dresses. We had so many come who had nothing. Often the first month was spent going to the dentist, and doctors. Catching up on shots and taking care of health issues that were neglected for long periods of time due to economic distress. We were so blessed to be helped by many in the health care system who knew that there was great need for each of these kids to be taken care of. I eventually got to know many of the Doctors on a first name basis. Many had a heart for our kids and would go the extra mile for them when they had needs. We would travel great distances for good dental care and special needs that could not be met close by. We had several girls come to us with broken teeth and were so blessed to see a dentist step up and fix those teeth for only what the insurance would pay and no more. The smiles that came as a result often would have the whole staff in the office crying as they watched the girls smile for the first time. I would then retake their pictures and put new ones on the wall. They just loved that. I did too! I would often have to teach about personal hygiene. I loved teaching them about what products to use to help their hair shine and them to smell pretty. It was a challenge to find products for each one that would be the best for their skin and hair. When they finally caught on they would blossom and we would love seeing the femininity of each one come to the fore front. They did as well. Getting six to eight girls out the door on school mornings was like herding cats!!!!!!!!!!!! The mirrors in the upstairs bathrooms were often crowded with girls curling hair and putting on make-up. My philosophy was that I wanted them to use colors that living folks would wear. I did not want them to be "gothic", or paint so much stuff on their eye lids that they could not fully open their eyes. I would stress that it was about enhancing their natural beauty not painting a new face on.

We had some tug of wars about my standards and I knew it would be hard at first. I had a few rules about street clothes. I had them bend over and if I could see parts of their behinds that should be covered they had to change. (No cheeky peeky). The shirts had to cover them up and be modest. Their skirts and dresses must cover them up when the girls bent over. Their clothes could not be skin tight or we would remove them from their possession. The girls and boys went to school together and I wanted to remove as many distractions as possible during their time together. I was not well received by the new girls, however as time went by they began to realize it was about what was best for them and not about me. Bill would often offer to go and buy some new clothes for them and that was incentive enough for them to conform. What they did not know about my husband is that he has great taste in women's clothing. I had some difficult times when we were enforcing these new standards on the girls. You might think I was being harsh and unfair however in the end it was about protecting them from unwanted advances and looks. We could not monitor what went on when they were at home. Eventually the girls who lived with us the longest came to appreciate that we loved them and wanted to protect them.

After one "coming to Jesus" evening at the house the girls were still upset and we asked them to sit with us at the table and talk. Bill looked at them with tears in his eyes and told them that we were not here to fight with them, but rather to fight for them. One girl began to cry hard and finally said no one had ever fought for her before. We realized that we had finally seen a break in her defenses and knew that she was going to be OKAY It would often takes months for the girls to come to trust us enough to begin to let go of the hurt she was carrying inside her for so very long. We also knew that things were going to get worse before they would get better.
However we were ready for that process and welcomed it. We tried to make Jesus Christ the center of everything we did and

said. We were not always successful and the kids would pick up on it and not hesitate to tell us about it. If you don't have a sense of humor don't do this job for it will be what bridges angry words and deeds to the love of Christ and His sacrifice for you.

We were always on alert when the girls were all upstairs and often would have to have them come back down to the Great Room so that the crazy monster would not strike when we were not looking. That is just what happened on this particular day. It was quiet for a while and I thought maybe they had all laid down to take a nap. No such luck! Suddenly there was hysterical laughter and running up and down the upstairs hallway. I went upstairs to investigate what had transpired and found to my amazement that they had taken tampons with applicators and painted the tips and turned them into rockets. They were shooting each other and running and hiding! I was counting the cost of the tampons already discharged and called a halt to that particular escapade.

Later that month we had the same scenario with all quiet then raucous laughter. The girls came to get Hannah and me, and we went into one of the girls rooms. They had placed underwear on the ceiling fan and turned it on. The air was full of laughter as well as bras and undies. I allowed it as there was not one hurt and they seemed to find it so funny. No harm done and the laughter was good and healthy. Finding ways to play with them and let them was always something we were looking for. We would often take them all to a park and let them play in the playground equipment. They had such a great time and there was an opportunity for them to just be kids. Enough of their lives had been spent in dealing with adult problems and adult consequences, that to find a place and time for them to let loose was vital for them to be able to do.

I like to play like the next person but we had a few girls that could beat me at any card game you name. It got to be a source of teasing for me when they wanted to play cards. I would like to say that I let them win but that wouldn't be the truth. That's okay with me, I loved to see their competitive natures come out, and they were not afraid of retribution from any of the staff if they did win. That was not always true in their home life.

Learning to drive was a privilege that our kids were not necessarily going to have on Ranch, until my husband stepped up to the plate. He decided that he would teach the older girls how to drive so that they could get their driver's license at some point in the future. We had a three girl rule when they wanted to go. We learned that two girls could cook up a story and stick to it but three would make that much harder. They had to have their home-work done and be doing well in school. They all wanted to learn and we had an old Ford F150 pickup truck that we used at Serenity Valley for farm chores, so he used that. We lived in the mountains and the roads were narrow and often had no shoulder to speak of. So when he would leave I always had a prayer meeting for them and for him especially! I trusted him and knew that he would be calm and cool with whatever happened. The girls were a different story and often when they would come back one or two would be white as a sheet, and couldn't wait to tell me their harrowing stories. They were never as bad as they said but you must know by now that DRAMA is the key word in a household filled with teen age girls. Bill did find out one or two needed glasses so we undertook to get that taken care of before the next driving lesson. Some did really well and some needed to practice for many more hours. He would always make a way to take them driving, if they had met the criteria. Once again he is my hero and the only man I have ever loved. I would rather clean toilets than take teenage girls driving! It is good to know one's limitations. He would set a girl down when they got back if he had experienced problems with them listening and following instructions. They were not allowed to drive until they proved themselves trustworthy. It was a big deal to be able to go with him. He took many girls over our time there and helped them study for their written driving tests. We were so proud when they passed!

Chapter Eight – A Family Ministry

Early on in our time at Serenity Valley one of the men on senior staff told Bill about what his role in this ministry would be. He said that Bill would be practicing the ministry of "Presence". That so much of the hands on stuff would fall on me and he would not be able to participate. That would prove to be the truth over and over again. He would sit in his chair if I had to go upstairs and handle a situation. He would listen to crying girls and frustrated RIs. He is not perfect and would lose his temper but not before being pushed to beyond human limits. The girls who were with us for years came to love him and call him Dad. He loved them with everything he had and would do everything in his power to protect them. When things heated up we had a pass word that I would use to tell him I wanted him to intervene, I had to use it from time to time and was glad to know that he had my back,

He is a Godly man and was challenged and tested beyond belief by our time there at the Ranch. He would stand between his girls and the boys, he would become a great big marshmallow when they would hug him or share triumphs with him. He submitted to having his hair gelled and styled, makeup applied liberally and loved the fashion shows that would come when the girls would get new clothes. He would remind them that they were daughters of the King of Kings and that they were loved unconditionally. It was a hard concept for an abused girl to process that they were so completely loved. We attempted to demonstrate that by our attitudes and actions during their time at the Ranch. I hope and pray that many believed it and will continue to do so the rest of their lives. If that takes place we have scored a victory against the evil one. He would light up when they would come home from school and share their day with him. He takes the time when we are in restaurants to talk to the waitresses or cashiers about God and His love for them. He does not want to miss an opportunity to proclaim the love of Christ. He misses the kids to this day as do I. We were living out a dream that we had to be able to help kids come to Christ and not end up in prison. We know that some have given their lives to Christ and live for Him. Glory to God!

When we left Michigan he had worked at the electric cooperative for almost 26 years. He started as a grounds man and had worked his way up to being the General Manager. He is smart, and a problem solver, he was very respected by those who worked for him, and by those in the community where we lived. When we went into ministry is was as if we had never accomplished anything up to that day. It was hard to be treated as the "help" and we experienced that in many ways over the years we were in "full time" ministry. In other words living where we were serving. Being mistreated is not new in ministry, it was just new to us. Frustration and anger are a result of being ground down over and over again. He was a systems analyst and would create ways of doing things that did not take the time or human effort that had been expended by the previous process. Then being told they "liked" doing things that way and refused to listen and change. This brought anger and frustration. We are both kids from the Detroit area and the "car company" mentality was "get it done right and faster". That was how we were raised. It seemed as if we never did have the collateral needed to be heard. He was even told one time to keep his ideas to himself they were neither needed nor wanted. This level of disrespect was prevalent in the world we had found ourselves living in. When it would all come to a head we were chastised for being upset. This brings great despair and discouragement to your soul and spirit. We were told before we ever left Michigan that we were going to be administering the Serenity Valley Ranch. Later we were to find out this was a lie.

We had poured our retirement savings into Serenity Valley as there were expensive repairs needed that the Ranch did not have the funds for. Equipment needed replacing as it was no longer safe to use. Screens for windows, wiring, plumbing, vehicles and equipment for lawn maintenance. We bought bikes and sports equipment. Took the kids on outings and helped where ever we could. The funds were just not there to keep things working and safe and so we pitched in. We believed we would be there and retire there. We were all in, emotionally, physically, financially, and spiritually. God knew this and we rested in Him, we were to come to know the greatest betrayal of our lives.

Our own family had joined the staff later in the first year we were there. It was such a huge blessing to have them there. We thought when we left their weddings that they would be settling in the North as the guys were from Wisconsin and Minnesota, and both loved their homes. We were fine with whatever they chose however as the year went by Jeff and Leigh Ann contacted us and said that the Lord was leading them to apply. They both became teachers on the main Ranch and were very active in the homes with the kids. They both loved kids and it was a great fit. Meredith and Amos came next and they would both teach as well as Meredith helping in the main office. They would stay a year and Amos would accept the position of Associate Pastor at the Fellowship Bible Church in Russellville. That would become the springboard for them to pursue becoming missionaries in Albania. We were also blessed to be present for the birth of all our grandchildren. Elijah was Jeff and Leigh Ann's first, then came Thad. Meredith and Amos had Isaiah and then Seth and finally our sweet Olivia Jane. Jeff and Leigh Ann left the Ranch after we did by a few months. Jeff is now teaching in Fort Smith Arkansas at South Side High School. He is to this day one of the best teachers I know for exciting the kids to learn and participate in that process. Leigh Ann is home schooling the boys and is busy with two babies as well. She and Jeff have become foster parents and are active in a ministry aptly named the CALL (Children of Arkansas Loved for a Lifetime). We are amazed at the faith of our kids and at their desire to love and serve God for a lifetime. They were very active at Serenity Valley, they all know the stress and trials of working with at risk teens, and they all loved their time working with the kids at the Ranch. We loved having them there as well and seeing our grandkids growing was also a blessing, We are now separated by thousands of miles as God has moved us back to Michigan. However with the help of technology we can Skype and see the kids and grandkids as well.

Chapter Nine – Fences Around the Pasture

Talking about the school at Stormharbor reminds me of the fun we had when it would snow in the mountains. They would cancel school and all the Ranch turned out for snow ball fights, sledding down the hill in laundry baskets and building snowmen. We would laugh right out loud at the crazy things the kids would find to slide down the hills on. With dogs running around barking and kids screaming, and laughing it was a great fun. We would have them come in and dry off and have hot chocolate. It was a memory making event in every aspect. We adults could not resist being kids for the day and sledding too. I have to say that my fifty something body did not respond as well to the bumps as it did when I was a kid. However that never did stop me from playing right along with them whenever the chance presented itself. I would just use pain cream the next few days afterwards. The one weather system we did not want to ever see was ice. That was a dangerous and often deadly event in the mountains. It seemed that it would happen every few years, and life ground to a halt. Serenity Valley was seven miles away from the main campus at Stormharbor and we would not risk the drive to go for school or chapel as long as the roads were icy. That was a big disappointment for the kids as they really enjoyed the interaction with the boy's houses and other staff and missed them when we were forced to stay home. Sometimes we would lose power and the roads became impassable. The first year we had no back up for the power. Later a generator would be installed in the pole barn that would provide enough juice for us to turn on lights and heat as needed. The pole barn also housed Bill's workshop. It was his hideaway when needed and provided a place for us to lock up tools. There was also another temperature controlled room for gas and other toxic chemicals that needed locking up. Both of these rooms were added after we got to Serenity Valley. Needless to say as soon as it warmed up the ice melted and we had clean up afterwards for some time as many tree branches would break under the weight of the ice.

Serenity Valley had 39 acres and we were only using about two for the buildings that were there. There was a pond and more land that would be perfect to build two more girls homes on. We would often sit and dream about a lamp lighted drive, and more beautiful landscaping and the other girls that desperately needed a place like Serenity Valley to come and heal and be loved on. We shared that dream whenever we were asked to speak in pubic about the needs and future plans for Serenity Valley. There were many who were interested in investing in that dream and we were encouraged that in the future Serenity Valley would be as active a facility as Shiloh Valley. We knew without a doubt that there would be no shortage of girls who would be in need of this ministry and we knew that God would bring the house parents and other staff that would be needed to do it right. We were to never see that dream come to fruition, however at that time we had only dreams and wishes for more homes.

The need for safe residential homes is at an emergency level in our nation. Kids who have fallen through the cracks in our foster system, kids in juvenile facilities and others who have to remain in danger because there are just no beds in which to place them. We were working in a facility that did not take kids who were drug abusers, or violent. Often we would realize that there was some element of these things in their lives but were able to bring them in anyway. Other facilities were set up for these types of kids, we were not. We did not lock the kids in at night and wanted there to be a feeling of home away from home. We would eventually have to lock up the kitchen knives and then the kitchen itself as we had incidents where things done would bring the safety of the girls in peril. For the most part we were able to keep things open and free for them. We cannot be everywhere and have to be able to trust to some degree that the girls would not hurt each other. We had an office at the Lodge and all the medications were under lock and key and the office was locked as well. During the day we kept the office open if we were in it otherwise it was locked. We would conference in this office with two of us and a girl, if there was a need to be discrete.

Home visits most always posed a problem for the staff. We were sending kids back to a place where they were not always safe or cared for. The tension would rise as the time drew near for parents to arrive or the transport from DHS would arrive. We would encourage them that they would be alright, and that we would be there when they came home. We knew that we would probably have a week or so of bumpy behavior after they were on a home visit. Not all kids, not all homes, however enough of it happened that we often dreaded home visits as the kids would come home depressed and angry that things had not gotten any better at home while they were away. We had to talk to them about the fact that just because they had changed, their home environment had not. That is so hard to witness. Their folks had not come to know Christ and the kids so wanted that to happen. They wanted the "happily ever after" that comes with fairy tales. We knew that until they were further down the road they would not understand that their parents often had been abused as well and their souls and spirits were wounded and needed the Great Physician to heal them. We would pray for them and encourage the girls to talk about their faith when they went home. We had a few whose parents would bully them, or be sarcastic about the changes that had occurred as a result of their new walk with Christ. That was so hard to witness, and so we had to be ready to build them back up and love on them when they came back. We had kids leave for good and then contact us to say that they did not realize how good it was to be there until they had left and were faced with the lives they now had. We have kept in touch with many of them to this day. I rejoice when we hear that they are living for Christ and that they are raising their children in Christian homes. We did have not magic formula for loving on kids and leading them to Christ. We just tried to remain consistent and loving and ready to listen to them. We would go to the front porch and rock and hear all about what happened at home and what was on their hearts. We knew that they would have to process through the hurt and pain again and again until they found peace. Often that would take a very long time and with some it would never come while they were in our care. Our constant prayers were for them to come to have a loving relationship with Jesus Christ for a life time.

One of the best days of the whole school year is of course the last day. It is called a field day and there are tons of ways that the staff have fun ready for the kids on that day. There are games and races, and water fights and of course the annual "mud pit"! That huge hole in the first pasture that was filled with water. Tug of war and other games end up with a team getting mud from top to bottom. Along the way much of the staff ended up in similar fashion. A good time is had by all and the kids are laughing and having a ball. I tried to stay as far back from the craziness as was humanly possible, Bill however was caught right in the middle and so we had to hose him and the girls off before we could load them in the van for the ride back to Serenity Valley. We all slept well that night and ended up with quite a bit of laundry to do the next day.

Laundry was never anyone's favorite Chore and many kids were never taught what to do. We had tutorials whenever a new kid would arrive. We could not count on the fact that anyone else had taught them. We still found out that many were just shoving all their clothes into the washing machine pouring in the soap and closing the lid. It was a miracle that any machines were running in the homes. I heard from the boy's house parents that they were just as bad or worse. Hannah would often finish up the kids laundry while they were at school. She would do things for them all the time like that. I know many appreciated it, as did I. She would put the different piles on the end of the dining room table so that the kids could pick them up after school on their way to their rooms. I can't tell you how many times we had to run them back downstairs to pick up their stuff. If I did not know better I would tell you that it was invisible to them, along with the hundreds of other items that I would place there for them to take back to their rooms. When you have six to eight kids they cannot all leave things in the Great Room or it would resemble a rummage sale. If I had told them to take it up stairs and they ignored me, and I told them again, and again they did not follow through. I would confiscate the item and they had to do a chore to get it back. That worked pretty slick because I would save some of the more annoying chores for such an event. There was a period of time when I gave much grace for the kids to learn how we did things at Serenity Valley. I know that others often referred to us as strict and too structured, however I found that giving kid's boundaries actually gave them more freedom to both learn and fail and then succeed in an amazing way. Each girl would have to spend time cooking with me. Each would learn the way I wanted things done and then take the ball and run with it.

    We had a discussion one day with one girl in particular that thought I was too strict. She loved horses and had just finished putting the fence up in the back pasture the previous weekend. We asked her why we would fence the pasture land. She looked at us like we were crazy but responded that we did so to keep the horses safe and still give them room to roam and graze. I asked her if she thought we were being mean to the horses not letting them run free. Again she looked at me like I had two heads and said no, that they needed the structure and they would not get hurt by cars or wild animals when they were in our barn and pasture. We then pointed out to her that we were following the same premise as the fence. We were giving them room to roam and to learn new things in life, while keeping them safe and well cared for. She was quiet for a moment and then said very softly that she finally understood us, somewhat. We had more moments with her as she struggled to find peace in the valley. Often times even in times of peace the girls were running away from the bad memories of the pain that was inflicted on them. The battle rages on for the hearts and lives of these young women.

For me, a usually demonstrative person, refraining from touching the girls in anyway was terribly difficult. I found though that if I waited and let them make the first move the emotion was usually genuine. I cannot tell you the number of ways I have been hugged and loved on by these kids. There is the first way which is the running and jumping hug. This explosion of exuberance often resulted in us both nearly falling to the ground. With full size young women the fact that I held us both up was in and of itself a miracle. Then there was the sneak attack hug which was usually performed while coming up behind me and grabbing me around the neck and squeezing me until my eyes would bulge out of my head! There was also the "side hug" the only hug that the men on staff would give to a girl, in spite of their best efforts to control it often our kids would launch themselves at the men and give them a regular hug. We worked overtime to make sure there was never anything but genuine affection attached to our hugs. For kids who did not experience growing up, what the true love of a parent is like this can be a difficult thing to learn. Then there was the "you don't love me hug". Guilt being a great motivator such as it is, I did battle with that one so that I was not being manipulated by them. I was and still am one person who will avoid conflict at any cost and that particular character trait was tested and tested during our time in the valley. I found out much to my chagrin that I could not walk away from some conflicts and would have to use the Word of God that I had hidden in my heart to help me not to react to the provocation, instead I would have to thoughtfully respond to them, hoping and praying that along the way the Spirit of Peace would prevail in the trouble and we could talk our way through the issues. I had to use that same formula when parents would call and make accusations. I know that they were just responding from the place of their pain and so I would have to put my feelings on hold and listen to them so that I could respond with the love of Christ. I know that I would be hurt if my kids called another woman Mom, and so I must take into account their feelings in this matter, and find a way to build a bridge to her so that the kids were not caught in the middle and hurt more. It is a stunningly beautiful ballet to watch the Holy Spirit work healing in the lives of these girls, and to see how He mends the broken hearted, and brings peace and joy back into their lives. I was humbled to be a part of that glorious redemptive process that comes through our Lord Jesus Christ. In the meantime the keyword for working with teen age girls is DRAMA. We enjoyed an abundance of it and finally caught on that it is okay to let them be who they are within the confines of the home, and in so doing they were able to reconnect with the kid inside them that only wanted to be loved and protected, nurtured and disciplined, and released to find their way in the world without hurt and pain. We often had to wait a long time to see this happen. In the meantime we watched as they tried to function from a place of extreme woundedness using the tools they had crafted for themselves. We are all wounded in some way or another and find that we revert to that place unless we replace those head videos with the truth of God's Word. I would put scripture verses on the walls in the halls, on the walls in the Great Room, and on the sill of the kitchen sink. I knew that unless I would inundate our space with it we would not begin to learn it and use it as a weapon in the warfare we were in for the lives and hearts and souls and spirits of these beautiful young women.

      I spent many hours sitting next to the toilet listening to them scream and cry out from the pain that had made a huge tear in their souls due to abuse. I cannot even begin to describe the sound. It was a long and pitiful wailing that came from deep inside them. I so wanted to reach inside them and rip the memories from them, however that is something only the King of Kings and Lord of Lords can do. Healing comes from Him. I knew this intimately. So I would hold them and we would rock back and forth and I just let them cry until their tears were spent then we would talk. I am no hero in all of this we came because we were called by God to come. We stayed because we knew that our lives were making a difference in theirs. We left because there was no choice given us but to go.

Chapter Ten – Support From Others

All along the path of the journey God placed people who would minister to us and build us up and bring a smile of joy and laughter to our lives. I was blessed to be friends with just such a Lady. Her name is Tina and she owns and operates a small beauty shop. The first time I met her I felt an immediate connection soul to soul with her. Her smile comes from deep inside her and she loves with great ferocity. I went to her shop because the other ladies on the Ranch had highly recommended her and they were not wrong. She is very good at cutting hair, however that was not her calling in that small shop in town. Her calling was to love on you, pray for you, build you up, correct your thinking, and then send you back with peace and strength. You see she is a child of God that watches and prays for opportunities to share her faith, to come along side you and build you up. She would give our girls haircuts and not charge us, instead she would sit a girl in the chair and begin to complement them on their beauty. She knew that they did not see that person when they looked in her mirror, however that did not deter her from lovingly washing their hair, combing it and styling it into something that complemented them in every way. I know that as she was putting her hands on their shoulders she was praying for them, for healing and peace, for joy and to come to a saving knowledge of the Lord Jesus Christ. She and I would eventually come to an agreement and I would teach her piano lessons and she would do my hair. I got so much more than I ever gave in that arrangement. I would limp into her shop and she would begin to minister to my spirit. She was a prayer warrior for the girls on the ranch. We would often pray together before she ever did my hair. She was for me a breath of fresh air driven by the Holy Spirit of God. I would later learn that she struggles with her health and yet there was never a word of complaint or trouble from her. I know that when we finally all get to heaven I will search her out again and let her know that her faithfulness to me and the girls was truly a gift from the arms of our Heavenly Father.

We were so blessed to have another dear friend of the Ranch. Her name is Mayanna, and she was a fierce defender of the ministry. She was a Yankee like us and we made an instant and loving connection with her and then her husband as well. She would motivate women from her church to become partners with us. They were so very faithful to us and the girls. Parties and Christmas presents, their time and love. Mayanna was very savvy in the business world and helped us to find our way around in making ourselves known in the surrounding communities. She would eventually work to have the Ranch receive an award through her tireless efforts to promote us and help us to find other ways of funding. The Ranch was mostly funded by donations and we had very lean times when there was not enough to pay the staff and keep the kids. The Ranch most often would take kids who had no visible means of paying for the room and board. These kids needed a place as did many others. We wanted there to be a half and half situation but we were not policy makers and often our input was scorned. So we made connections on our own with those who had a heart for wounded girls. She was one of our champions and we could not have imagined how much she would get done on our behalf. The girls never really understood that they were there and being taken care of due to the love and support of God's people like her. We were to see her and Larry several times after we left the Ranch. We count them among the many gifts that God gave us during our time at Serenity Valley.

The house parents that were on the Ranch would become an invaluable part of our support system and dear friends. We would first become friends with Jenny and Gerald. They were from Texas and had first come to the Ranch for Gerald to help with maintenance on the vehicles. Instead they became houseparent's in a boys' house. They had two boys of their own that they had on Ranch with them throughout that time. We were relief for them when we first arrived on Ranch and then again throughout that first year before we took in girls. Jenny and I loved spending time together. Often we would take a trip to Hot Springs to get groceries and stop at the Hot Springs National Park and get a 25 dollar massage and have a cheap lunch. We would talk all the way down and back up the mountain. Cry together, laugh together and know that we would always be friends. To this day we are in touch. Jenny and Gerald left the boys ranch to go to work at another facility in Texas. Now they are retired from child care, but their hearts are always going to be connected to the ministry of caring for wounded boys.

Darryl and Leanne were also house parents for the boys' ranch. They came from Colorado. Darryl had worked with at risk kids there and Leanne just had a heart as big as Colorado. We loved them right away they were humble gentle people who wanted to provide an environment that would encourage the boys to come to trust them and then to trust the Lord and Savior they served. We know that they were all in when they came as were Jenny and Gerald. We all put more than ourselves into our work there, we spent our retirement funds and then some of our pay checks for the things that the kids needed.

Bobby and Mara were there as well. They were very young compared to the rest of us and they house parented the little guys. They loved what they were doing and they did it well. However along the way they realized it was not a safe environment for their young son. They stayed and worked on the Ranch in other areas. There was never any question that they loved the kids. They took us old Yankees in right away and there was never any prejudice towards us, just loving acceptance. We keep in touch with them to this day as well.

There were others there that came and went during our time there. Of course we were the only house parents for a long time for girls then came Matt and Julie. They were great folks who had such a love for kids. That seemed to be the case across the board for those who came on staff working in direct care. However their house was on the Boys Ranch and there were a few others that took girls in because we did not have room. We were the only ones at Serenity Valley. So the disconnect was there between the life they had and the one we lived. There were always people around on the Boys Ranch. It was a bigger operation and needed a good number of folks just to keep that small city a float. Water system, cattle ranching, horse ranching, equine therapy, fixing the vehicles that folks would donate to the ranch, picking up donations, keeping up with the maintenance of the homes and offices and out buildings as well as the small subdivision of mobile homes that housed other staff. There were the teachers and the numerous volunteers that came and went. We had a cafeteria that would feed everyone their lunch during the school year. It was truly an amazing feat to keep it all running. Into all this mix the house parents were expected to work outside their homes at least 20 hours a week. You might ask me, when did we have time to do that? Well, since we were the only ones keeping Serenity Valley running we worked more than twenty extra hours a week. We did not then turn around and work at Shiloh Valley as well. There were so many characters there when we were there and many more who will forever live in our hearts as gifts from our heavenly Father.

Of course there were conflict among the adults on Ranch. We were all human beings who were often under great pressure and acted out of that to the detriment of relationships. However almost everyone was willing to forgive and rebuild and start again working side by side for the kids. We cannot ever make everyone happy and saying that brings up memories of times we were on the receiving end of hurt and pain for no good reason. It is hard to fight against someone who has a beef with you but will not come and work it out face to face. We were not then nor are we now perfect, and mostly wanted there to be a team atmosphere in more than words, however that was not always the case.

People and relationships are stressed at the best of times but with the Ranch being mostly funded by donations, when the economy cratered we keenly felt that. There was a change in the administration and the way things were done dramatically changed with it. We went from a time of having a director who was proactive in fund raising, to one who believed that he was called only to pray and to sit and wait for God to provide the needs of the kids and Ranch. We struggled with having to leave the church we had attended in favor of one that was closer and took less gas to attend. We saw cut backs in staff pay and other issues arose as we still had kids to care for but no clear direction as to what that was going to look like. We were given one program to follow and then a few months later that fell by the wayside in favor of something completely different. Morale fell to an all- time low at that point. We just want to have strong leadership and set a course and follow it. We were pushing ahead with building relationships in the neighboring communities and had several folks express an interest in building new houses at Serenity Valley. This was a time of such emotional and spiritual confusion for those of us who had seen things start to happen that we knew would not have a good outcome. The flow of needy kids did not stop just because the economy was in such bad shape. We still had kids come and leave and more follow them. We saw a transition happening that we knew would not lead to a good outcome. We decided to knuckle down and pray our way through this believing that God had called us to this ministry and we were to spend the rest of our lives serving Him there. This would later become a source of huge pain and suffering for us and our family. We held tightly to the belief that if God called you to it He would see you through it. We knew that.

For we know that all things work together for good to those who are the called according to His purpose. - Roman 8:28

Chapter Eleven – Camel Kisses

    In the meantime life went on and we were taking new girls and finding the challenges and joy of each new one we took. We had one girl come and stay less than a week. We had others come and stay for months and some for years. We were finding ourselves in a comfort zone that we never believed we would accomplish given all that had transpired before. Lest you believe we did not have bumps we had two kids leave in the night and take our golf cart and go to the boys ranch where two boys climbed out their windows in the night to meet them. We would later find out that the golf cart died on the way back and it was snowing and cold, and they had to walk in the dark back home. We found that we had to dismiss girls. We tried as hard as we could to show grace and mercy however when there was danger involved we had to act decisively and remove that girl before greater harm was done.

    There was an internal struggle to be heard when things got really bad with a girl. We were assured that if we had a girl who was not going to work and we told them we needed her removed, that they would listen to us and do what was necessary to keep the home environment safe for the others by removing that girl. We would give second and third chances for the girl to make the necessary changes, often months would go by without any visible change and we would lay the ground work for the senior staff to see that we needed to make this change. It was still a traumatic event when we finally had to put our foot down. Often this would result in close examination of our motives and this was a painful process eroding the trust that had been built. The line that would wound us so deeply was " if you just loved her more", we were stunned that those words were spoken. There were going to be kids we were not set up and trained to take and keeping them with us just kept them away from the very therapy that would give them a chance to heal. I would like to say that as a Christian facility we were all pulling together however we are all uniquely human and so bring our "stuff" to the table when there are times of deep testing. I did love them each and every one, there were those however who were very hard to like. God gave us an extra measure of grace when we took those girls.

During this period of time our oldest daughter and her husband were living and working on the boy's ranch. They informed us that they were expecting our first grandchild. We did not find out it was a boy until the day he was born. We were overwhelmed with joy and anticipation at the arrival of this newest member of our family. God brings great joy in the midst of great trials. Our other daughter and her husband had accepted a calling to Fellowship Bible Church in Russellville and left the Ranch. This town was about thirty five miles away from the Ranch so we had to make a plan to see them. It was the first step in a journey for them that would eventually lead them to the mission field in Albania.

Joy mixed with pain was the daily recipe at the Ranch we had been there houseparenting and working for three years now. The national average is eighteen months. We were anxious to begin to build up Serenity Valley. There was a great desire in the churches we visited to see a place for wounded girls. We met so many women who had been abused and there had been no place for them to go. They were compelled to help financially to build up Serenity Valley and add new houses. There was not that same vision however from the new administration. There was no desire on their part to follow through with the promises that were made to us by the previous director and so we began to realize we may not see Serenity Valley become all that we believed it could be. We were even asked if we thought we could bring the girls over to the boy's ranch and live there. All that I now knew about abused girls and their need for safety and peace told me that living on the boy's ranch would not be healthy for them in the long run.

While not privy to the extent of the financial difficulties that the Ranch was experiencing, we did know that the times were difficult and yet we were at peace with the knowledge that God would provide for us and the kids as He had always done. We became a bit more proactive with getting the news of the tough times back to our church and friends and family, as they were great prayer warriors for us and the kids. There would be a letter of encouragement and tucked inside was a check for us. This would come from those least able to afford it and also from those who had pledged support for us and were faithful to follow through. We knew that these were God's kids and He loves them and wants to care for them. We also knew that this was stretching our faith in way we had not ever experienced before. Bill and I learned to walk by faith and not by sight! We knew that God would provide all our needs, not necessarily our wants. We were to find out over the years we were in full time ministry in Arkansas that we could live on very little and be just fine. Our health did suffer greatly while we were there however because we had no health insurance a great deal of the time and so let things go that maybe we should not have. God will have to sift through all that in the long run. We were able to get the kids what they needed and so we were proactive to keep them well and taken care of.

For my God shall supply all your needs according to His riches in glory through Christ Jesus. - Philippians 4:19

Some of the sweetest times on Ranch were chapels and prayer meetings with the staff. We could feel the presence of God so many times when we were in great distress or deep sadness. We found common ground at the foot of the Cross of Christ. I know that those years stretched my prayer life and built and rebuilt all that I had known and held dear about walking the Christian life. I know now that those were formative years and years that they would sift all that I was sure about. In its place was a closer and sweeter relationship with Christ and with my husband and family. My daughters and their spouses were proactive to support Bill and I and the girls we took care of. They would come over and play with the kids as well as help us when we needed extra hands.

I know that we all were there for the same reason, and that was we loved kids and wanted to step into the gap in their lives and offer them love and stability and a place to come and heal. We saw the love over and over with many on staff, both houseparent's, and support staff. I never doubted that God had called us to that ministry and to this day it is what I know deep inside me. We would later find out that often others who you thought were there to support you and build you up, would take any chance to shoot you in the back. We would describe this process as friendly fire. In Christianity is seems to be accepted and forgiven without penalty. I found that I was happier staying at Serenity Valley, maybe you could say I was hiding out. I prefer to describe it as being safe. We all came to the Ranch with emotional baggage and our own hurt and pain. Taking care of these kids would often bring up wounds from our own lives that we needed to take to the Great Physician and be healed from. It is not a magic pill and often there was not instant healing, however when we were willing God would start the process of anointing that past pain with His love and healing. We would be essentially walking the same road as our kids were and in that there is a bond formed that would enable us to say without fear of contradiction that we understood their hurt and pain, as we had lived it ourselves. That often would open up a dialog that would lead to the Word and the healing process would begin in their lives. You see nothing we have lived through is ever wasted by God. He uses it for our good and ultimately for His glory. I wanted to be broken and used for the sake of these girls and not walk away from this experience wishing I had done more or said more. I think as I write this book that I had accomplished much of what I went down there to do. As we walked out that journey we often wondered what the outcome would be and in the long run if we were alive to see some of the fruits of our labors. We are seeing the fruits and are blessed to be in communication with a lot of the girls we were able to serve and love during our time at Serenity Valley. God is so good to allow that in our lives at this time. Some of the girls are married and have children, some are not married and have children. There is no condemnation in that statement it is simply a fact. We have been blessed to be kept in the loop of their lives and to be the recipients of their news both good and bad. God is still working and we are seeing it all the time.

    We were blessed to have the neatest ministry right in our backyard so to speak, Heifer International's mission is to work with communities to end world hunger and poverty and to care for the Earth. They had on their grounds the different animals that were gifted to villages to begin herds that would bring income and sustain the population. They also had built villages that resembled the different countries that they were in. They had an open-house and we took the girls on a bright and sunny day. We toured the villages and saw the animals that were around the farm. We then went into the barns and were introduced to the different animals that were in there. One of the guides was talking about the camels that they had housed there and challenged the girls to feed the camels. Well needless to say our most daring rose to that challenge, however we were to find out quickly he wanted them to put the apple in their mouths and give it to the camel that way. Right away we lost more than half of our volunteers and I was not surprised, but we did have a few more daring that stepped up to the plate. We stood ready with camera in hand as the first girl held the apple in her teeth and the camel leaned in and with his two incredibly huge lips practically covered her face retrieving the apple from her mouth. We all gasped at the size and flexibility of his lips and also at the saliva he left in his wake! Yikes I thought for sure there would be no more takers after that demonstration. Again I was wrong and our toughest girl stepped up to the guide and placed her apple in her mouth, she had not even turned back when that huge animal swooped in and massaged her face with his lips coming away with the prize and leaving behind a huge sloppy kiss on her face. We were all laughing so very hard by then as we could not imagine anything grosser than having camel spit all over your face. I know now that the challenge, whatever it was, became the fuel for some pretty spectacular stunts that we were to be front row spectators to. Never challenge a camel to a duel with your lips, he has you beat before you start because of the size of his! I have pictures of that day and so even if they deny it now, I can prove that they kissed a camel.

Bill and I were always thinking about what we could do to help them be more productive and begin to feel a part of our Serenity Valley family. The kids were always wanting to ride mowers and drive tractors and trucks. So he decided that they could learn to mow the lawn. Well having decided that, we talked to them and asked them if they had ever done yard work and driven a garden tractor. The immediate response was always yes. We were new at this so we believed them. That was our first mistake! They did not know what they were doing and they drove the mowers into the ditches and across huge rocks and into the fields, one girl even drove over a stump and got caught on top of it! We were then in the position of having "how to" classes for the equipment. We had some "girly girls" and our share of "tough girls". This did not stop the competitions that ensued whenever there was an opportunity. It would be quite common to look out and see one driving and two riding in the garden wagon behind her. Again it was as much about learning to play as it was about working. We tried to team them up so that they could learn cooperation and sharing. That always presented us with a new set of issues depending on how many of them were taught to share. We could teach some pretty effective life lessons when there was one who would not carry her load and the others wanted to do the job well. When you raise children from an early age you can watch their strengths and weaknesses and begin to guide and direct them toward things that will enhance the gifts that they have. When you get them as young teens you have a definite disadvantage in that process. So if a young girl liked music and wanted to learn we would look at how we could facilitate that desire. The same with many things that they would say they were interested in. Obviously we had a disadvantage in that we did not keep most of them for many years, it was usually months to a year at the max. So we had to be a bit quicker to recognize and feed the creative processes. We loved it when they would write a story or sing a song that they had written. We were delighted in their creativity and the drive it took to accomplish that task. We praised them liberally and pushed them to work harder to build and develop the skills that we had fostered in them. God would give us great guidance as well as the teachers and other staff who would work with them. We worked best as a team and when that worked well it was something to behold. The girls would feel enveloped in the love that came from each and every one who worked for their healing and health.

    I am a musician and have been many years now. I play the piano and I taught piano in Michigan for 26 years. The ranch found an old baby grand piano that had taken a beating but was "donated" to the Ranch. They placed it in the Great Room at the Lodge. I had brought a lot of music with me from Michigan and so I would bring things over and sit down in the evenings during homework and quiet time and begin to play. I played mostly sacred music but I had books of movie scores as well as a bunch of classical music. It has been proven over and over that music can bring down blood pressure and relax nerves, sooth and calm, and bring great peace. I can say that was the case for us at the Ranch. As I began to play, kids would come down stairs and sit around the room with their homework, they were quiet and calm and peaceful. Quite often they would ask me to play, and as time went by they would all have their favorites. I hear back from time to time from them and many say that they wish they could hear me play the piano again. What a God we serve who knows what it takes to speak to our souls and to bring peace to our hearts. His provision throughout those years never failed us and His grace and mercy were apparent each and every day.

Chapter Twelve – Daughters to the King of Kings

Woven through the tapestry of these years was the love God has for each of us. His mercies were new every morning and in spite of man's best efforts to cause hurt and pain, God showed himself faithful. We were often so unprepared for the drama that would ensue over the silliest things, yet it was such a great illustration of what God must see among His children each and every day. Being in "ministry" does not provide you a special dispensation from troubles among the folks. In fact if it does anything it magnifies it. Different personalities and belief systems, different language, customs, and levels of spiritual maturity. When you begin to factor that into the everyday workings of a home for kids you have yourself a recipe for trouble with a capitol T. So navigating those issues with the kids as an audience was tricky at best. We knew that whatever we did or said was being observed and processed for future usage. Oh boy did you hear about it again if you lost your temper, and you will, that was a given. You needed to follow the gospel model and get it right as soon as possible. The evil one would use those times to drive a wedge between folks that could bring a whole house to a standstill. Learning to repair wrongs and build bridges was a never ending process. During that time in church our pastor was teaching a sermon series that he aptly titles "Allelon". The love one another series from the book of 1John.

Beloved, let us love one another, for love is from God; and everyone who loves is born of God and knows God.

The one who does not love does not know God, for God is love,

By this the love of God was manifested in us, that God has sent His only begotten Son into the world so that we might live through Him.

In this is love, not that we loved God, but that He loved us and sent His son to be the propitiation for our sins.

Beloved, if God so loved us, we ought to love one another.

No one has seen God at any time; if we love one another God abides in us, and His love is perfected in us. 1 John 4:7-12

God makes it abundantly clear to us all that love is how we are to function in this crazy world we live in. His way brings about peace and change, often though not before much hurt and pain have occurred. I know that God showed up in that series and brought some amazing tools for us to use in our relationships with each other. I am still referring back to those notes in my Bible today years after that teaching. We needed to walk our talk in front of those kids which included practicing the teachings on reconciliation. Restoring them into right standing with us and with each other so that there could be peace again in the house. We had girls come to live with us whose insides were in constant turmoil, and this would spill out into the house and cause unrest. We had to become very good at circumventing this process and bringing the Holy Spirits' power of discernment into the process of restoring the peace in the house. This is no small thing when you have open spiritual war fare in the house. Each new girl would bring into the house all that she had seen and experienced. We would then begin anew the process of finding out who she really was and how God could work in her life to bring her to Himself. Along the way there were times of laughter and joy as well as times when you would ask yourself if you had really been called of God to do this work. Introspection can often be a great tool to see where it is you need to begin working on your own "stuff". It was there you can be assured it will come out. However you had to function each and every day to take care of the girls and each other in spite of the pain you may be dealing with at that time. Compartmentalizing was a tool that you became very good at using. The idea that you will deal with it later was really just a myth because it would color your reactions and thinking until you took it to the Throne of God and laid it down at His feet begging Him to heal you and to give you peace. It might not come right away but in time you would feel that burden lifting and you could see clearer into the future because the past had been cleansed.

We traveled to Oklahoma to view the operations of a successful girls' ranch there. We learned all kinds of neat things and took the help they offered with great gratitude. We took their handbook and their rules and they were available to us to call whenever we needed to talk. We spent time that day with the director who had been there working for many years, he said that they sent their kids to local schools and every year or so one would end up pregnant out of wedlock. He finally sat the girls down and asked them what they could do different to help them stay pure until they were married. They replied that they were so poor they knew that they would never had a fairy tale wedding like other girls so they just gave up and gave in. He was shocked that he had not realized that this was what they were thinking and created an outside gazebo for weddings, there on campus. They had wedding dresses donated that were just beautiful and the Ranch paid for the reception and handled the service. After that the pregnancies were few and far between and the girls could come back even after leaving and have their weddings there. I latched onto that idea and started my own collection of wedding stuff. We planted crape myrtles of every color outside in the front yard in preparation for future weddings. I urged the girls to see themselves as God sees them, redeemed and pure in Christ. We had many who wanted to get married at Serenity Valley. I could not wait for those days to come to pass. We had a second purity program for the girls and they were given purity rings. God is the God of second and third chances and many more and we wanted them to know that it was not too late to live a chaste and pure life. To have a good and healthy and happy marriage. We wanted them to have all that God has in store for those who love them. Bill would tell them often they are "daughters of the King of Kings and Lord of Lord!" We had to repeat it over and over before they began to see themselves as God sees them. When they finally did it was a cause for great rejoicing and weeping tears of joy. I have been to that place with them and know the freedom and joy that is there. This was just another victory over the evil one who wanted to kill and steal their lives from them. We know who wins this battle and yet we have been on the front lines when there were battles that we lost. Girls who would for a time begin to believe that their lives had value and there was a loving heavenly Father who wanted them. Earthly fathers have often been the source of great abuse and so making that leap takes extraordinary faith and trust. Then they slip back into the lies' of the enemy and allow themselves to be swallowed up by his evil. I have wept myself to sleep many a night begging God to cover and protect them and knowing that their decisions would eventually lead to their deaths. God knows the situation intimately and yet their will comes into that battle and they are afraid of the changes believing that they cannot do it so they just quit trying. I know that my Redeemer lives and in that I rest my heart and life. I pray for them to this day that God would keep them safe. There has not been a day since we left there that I have not prayed for them and thought of them. I loved them then and I love them now, I was their Mom for the time they were there and many still call us Mom and Dad to this day. It is a title of honor that I am humbled to be addressed with.

Chapter Thirteen – Love and Tears

God alone knew what it would take to start that ministry and what the cost would be to us and to our health and marriage. We were so very blessed that during that time we were able to address issues in our own lives that brought our marriage to a new and stronger place than it had ever been in before. We have been married today nearly 37 years. I have never considered my life with anyone but Bill. God gave us to each other and we have held tight in spite of some very rocky times. God healed Bill and I, and changed us both through this whole process. Our daughters say that he is not the same man that they grew up with. I am so very blessed to have him in my life and to walk out our time here on this earth together. It is an amazing thing to take a man who was successful in the business world and highly respected there and in our community, and was actively involved in ministry here in Michigan and place him in the environment where folks treated him as one who had no value except to keep the place clean and running so that they could do ministry around him. It is a huge and often crushing thing to have someone tell you that your opinion was not needed or wanted. Yet we frequently were in that position. God was our only comfort when that situation arose as He alone knew our hearts and what we were there to do and capable of. We found that as the years went by that challenge got greater and more painful to work through. It would have been common sense that if you train someone to do a job, and they are there day in and day out, that they would gain the wisdom and experience to carry it out. However we were often treated like it was day one and we were not capable of making a well thought out, prayed out decision.

I am not sure if fear or anger or selfishness ruled these times. They were to get more frequent as the years waned that we were at Serenity Valley. We kept the house filled with girls throughout that time and were blessed immeasurably because we saw God show up in spite of human flaws. We saw Him move and work to provide all our needs just in time. Walking by faith and not by sight became the way we lived. We had spent the vast majority of our retirement savings setting up and running Serenity Valley, and what we did not spend there we lost when the market crashed in 2008. The world would have characterized it as a free fall, we knew that God was holding us up and would take care of us in the future as He had in the past. You see we learned that until you come to the end of yourself you will never let God do what He has promised to do.

He who did not spare His own Son but delivered Him up for us all, how will He not also with Him freely give us all things? - Romans 8:21

We had many opportunities to walk out those promises in front of the kids and see them begin to realize that God did have an active interest in every aspect of their lives and ours too. I loved to sit on the front porch and as I did the kids would filter out and sit next to me and we would begin to discuss how many ways God has been evident in their lives since they have been at Serenity Valley. The messages at chapel, the times around the family dinner table, the gifts and love sent to them from folks they had never met. It all culminated in an opportunity for me to teach them of the faithfulness of their Heavenly Father. That in spite of the evil ones desire to kill and steal and destroy, God almighty is still in control. He works through His people, through the creation, through the still small voice, through the power of His spoken Word. He makes Himself available to come to us and love us, and to lead us to the saving power of His only Son Jesus Christ. He who made the ultimate sacrifice of laying down His life, so that we might have salvation and power to live triumphant lives in this world. At the end of our earthly lives we have a life with Him in heaven in the next. I am no theologian but having spent fifty nine years on this earth, and having made the decision to live that in the power of Jesus Christ, I have had a front row seat to many miracles, and seen the power of God show up over and over. That is the only thing I place my hope and faith in. They were very clear about that from day one with us, until the time they left.

We had morning devotions every day after breakfast and before they left for school. Many times we were working through devotions written specifically for teenage girls. They were of a necessity not so deep that they could not comprehend them, rather we discussed topics such as modesty, purity, salvation, life in Christ and practical aspects that they could understand and sink their teeth into. We knew that it was vital for them to have all the strength and joy and peace that that time can bring into a day that would and often did turn out hectic and sometimes very painful. We worked hard to keep their home a sanctuary, to run to when the school day, or counseling, or other troubles threatened to overwhelm them. I was in the kitchen when they would get home from school and I could read their faces well enough to know if the evening was going to be quiet or turbulent. We would make ourselves available to them upstairs, and down, to listen and talk them through the stuff that happened. Hopefully as time went by they would begin to discern what was important and what needed to be let go in favor of a good night's sleep. Resolution and reconciliation was sought at all costs but often had to be delayed in favor of letting emotions subside and clear headedness prevail. I was blessed to watch them mature and begin to work through things as we had provided the environment for them to do. Forgiveness was often a very hard concept to accept. We would tell them that not forgiving their enemies was like them eating rat poison and expecting the other person to die. They could not grasp that concept at first as the wounds were often very deep seated and had been around a long time. Yet as they began to see the grace and mercy that Christ gave, and hopefully the same from the staff, they were able to begin the long process of letting God heal their hearts as they worked their way toward forgiveness. I cannot tell you that it was an easy process and that there were not setbacks. The staff would tell you that we are all on that journey in some way or another. We bring our hurts to the cross and we leave them there, only to grab it up on our way out. We have developed a comfort in having those hurts and keeping them close to us. The process of letting them go often can take years to accomplish. However in the meantime finding the grace to work on that stuff was one of the reasons we were at Serenity Valley. My deepest hope and prayer for each girl was that they would develop a love for the Lord Jesus Christ. That they would accept His love and sacrifice made on their behalf at the cross of Calvary. That they would live a life in freedom from the past, joyfully looking to the future that God has prepared for them who are His own. I want them to have the freedom that only a life in Christ brings and the power and victory to be effective in the battle for souls that is getting stronger and stronger each and every day. My hopes and desires for my own girls came into play for each of the girls of Serenity Valley. I wanted them to have all that God intended for them to have in this life and in the next.

Delight yourself in the Lord and He will give you the desires of your heart. Commit your way to the Lord, trust also in Him and He will do it. - Psalm 37:4-5

This is powerful confirmation that God is for us and wants us to have all that He has promised us in His word. The greatest gift that He gives us is peace, even in the midst of the worst hurt and pain, and the greatest trials.

Cast your burden upon the Lord and He will sustain you; He will never allow the righteous to be shaken. - Psalm 55:22

I would often quote these verses to myself and also to them as they approached a particularly difficult situation. Home visits were a source of great anxiety. Their families had not changed. The girls had found Christ and the peace and joy He brings and wanted to be the ones to bring their families to that same saving knowledge. Seldom did things turn out the way that they planned. Often home visits were painful and disappointing, even hurtful. There was criticism of their new found faith and negativity about their lives. Oh how I wanted to spare them this pain. I knew that when they got back we would have to be patient as they acted out their hurt and pain. We often silently wished we could skip that process all together. We did not however ever voice our feelings to the kids as that would then provoke the need for them to defend their families. We were not in competition for their affection.

I have to share a funny story about the vehicles that we had donated to the Ranch. We had been given a fifteen passenger van, a Ford pickup truck and a mini-van. We used the smaller vehicle for day to day running with just a few of us. We needed the bigger van for us all to go anywhere together. The truck was used for Ranch chores and hauling. The mini-van was in great shape when it arrived which really pleased us. Often folks donated vehicles that need work and have many miles on them. We get a year or so and then they are ready for retirement. This van looked good and we were glad. We began to notice some odd things as we drove it back from Conway one afternoon. Hannah was with me and the windshield wipers started, of their own accord! We were both stunned as the day was sunny and I had not touched the switch. Well after about a mile or so it stopped. We did not think much about it until one afternoon the lights came on inside and outside of the vehicle without us touching the switches. OKAY I told her we are dealing with something bigger than we first thought. I was out in the van alone and the horn started honking! I know the folks around me were startled as was I and quite perplexed. I took it home and told Bill to fill out a service request. We had issues and they were to get bigger. I would get into the car and put the key in the ignition and the drivers' seat would automatically lay itself all the way back, and the outside mirror would turn away from the window. Now I am not sure about you but I began to think we had a demon at work in this vehicle. We would be sitting in church and the horn would begin honking, Bill would see the ushers looking and automatically get up and go stop it. We were now quite wary about taking this car anywhere. Hannah and I got the manual out and began looking to see if we had a wiring issue. The manual told us that you can program the car to change seat positions and mirror positions for each driver. Well! I thought we can just change it back again if that was all that was happening. We decided to work on it after lunch. We got into the vehicle and she read the manual and followed the instructions. We did what they said and I put the key into the ignition and turned it and the seat laid down the horn honked and the mirror turned away from us. I tried again and again to reprogram the vehicle. By the time we had been at it an hour we were laughing so hard we were sick to our stomachs! One of Elizabeth Elliott's favorite sayings was dancing in my head... "With acceptance comes peace!" So we just learned to deal with the vans quirks and laughed when it did things we were not expecting. We prayed that anything evil would be removed and asked God to give us safety while driving it. He granted our requests and we used the van frequently. Who cares if the wipers started on an eighty degree and sunny day! The staff just said, well it is a "ranch vehicle". There were many vehicles donated that had quirks and we loved telling stories about them and what they did for the others who were to use them with glad hearts. We knew that it was saving the Ranch money when folks would donate vehicles. We did not have to purchase new ones that way.

    Many things were donated to help us. We would put it to good use and be glad for the money that was saved. I had washers and dryers, fridges, appliances, furniture, dishes, bikes and sports equipment towels and, bedding at the Lodge that were donated to help us provide a good and healthy environment for the kids. God's people meeting the needs of the Ranch as God placed it on their hearts. What a neat picture of family it was for the girls. We all got very good at seeing the hand and provision of the Lord come at just the right time and with just the right thing. I never got tired of showing the girls these things that were provided for them to have a safe and comfortable place to live

I knew that many of our kids came from homes that struggled financially, many had never had the comforts afforded them while they lived at the Ranch. However that did not deter them from wanting to go home and be with their families. We had kids come to us from out of state and that made getting them home logistically difficult and expensive. We made trips to Little Rock to the airport to put kids on planes and fly them back home for a visit. We spent one whole day at the Little Rock airport being told that the plane was delayed and would be there shortly, at the end of an eight hour day they told us it was broken and another would not be there until the next day. We were seventy miles from the Ranch. We would take them back and get up early and go back the next day. Somehow the Ranch found the money to pay for the tickets. We would be promised reimbursement and most often never saw any come. God knows. We knew that the connections that needed to be made were more important. There were cases where the connections were so hurtful for the kids yet there was a drive inside them to keep reaching out even when it was so damaging to them and to all the healing they had done to date. We were in the front row to see how damaged the relationships were and some continue to be. I was baffled as a mother myself to see the hurtful and hateful things parents can do to their kids over and over. I so wanted to spare the girls that hurt and could not do so. How much more my Heavenly Father sees this behavior in us toward Him and His Son. There were more illustrations of this than I can possibly recount. I would like to tell you that it got easier to let them go, however it did not. When we knew that they were going home for a visit we would spend more time in prayer petitioning the Heavenly Father to protect them, and to keep them, and that the time would be sweet and good for them. More often than not it was not that way. We got to see the generational nature of the hurt and pain that is visited on our families. We prayed that the girls would be the generation that would break the cycle of abuse, abandonment, and neglect. I have high hopes that many of the kids will indeed realize this prayer of mine in their lives.

> *For I am confident of this very thing, that He who began a good work in you will perfect it until the day of Christ Jesus. - Philippians 1:6*

This was a promise that I held close to my heart throughout the years we loved and lived with these girls. I know that God is able and willing to do just that very thing in willing hearts and lives.

Kids being kids we were always on the lookout for ways to give them an outlet for their energy. We bought a video game and the mat called "Dance, Dance, Revolution" for them to play with They could then put on the video and select a degree of difficulty and begin following dance steps to the music and see how many points that they could get before the music was finished. I had hours of amusement watching them practice their dance steps and try to keep up with the video. We even invited a boys' home over to have supper and a dance competition. What great fun that was. We had every level of proficiency in that room and it was competition at its finest. That was a great investment for our house and the girls used it and used it. When the weather was nice I would insist that they go outside and get some fresh air. We had bought hula hoops and games and balls and such to play with. There was a Bocce Ball game, there was a Croquet Game and Basketball court. We had purchased bikes of every size for them to ride on. We would find them hanging in the trees and sitting on the porch talking. It mattered not what they did as long as they were playing. During these times they would get along quite well. I was always amazed when there was an eruption that would set the house a blaze with hurt and pain. It was almost as if they could not stand the peace and quiet as it did not drown out the pain that was so loud in their souls. I could always tell when we were getting down the road toward healing as the girls would become much lighter and happier around home. They began to look past their own hurts and pains and reach out to others. I loved those times as it meant that God was hearing and answering our prayers on their behalf. We have to continually give Him the glory for all that was accomplished in the lives of the girls at Serenity Valley. Our position was to be available to them and to take care of their needs while God worked inside them to free them from the captivity of their pasts. It was a blessing to behold the newness that would result of the letting go and forgiving. We were to see that process repeated many times during our stay there. I count it among God's greatest gifts in my life. The bright face and light heart, the peace in knowing that there is now freedom that cannot be taken away. What a wondrous Savior and King we serve! The Word tells us in Isaiah that He has come to set the captives free. We got to be there and see that first hand.

The Spirit of the Lord GOD is upon me, Because the LORD has anointed me To bring good news to the afflicted; He has sent me to bind up the brokenhearted, To proclaim liberty to captives And freedom to prisoners; To proclaim the favorable year of the LORD And the day of vengeance of our God; To comfort all who mourn, To grant those who mourn in Zion, Giving them a garland instead of ashes, The oil of gladness instead of mourning, The mantle of praise instead of a spirit of fainting. So they will be called oaks of righteousness, the planting of the LORD, that He may be glorified.... - Isaiah 61:1-3

Indeed that was the mission of Serenity Valley to see this scripture fulfilled in the lives of each and every girl who came down the long winding driveway into the Valley. That there would be freedom for a lifetime through faith and life in Christ. We had no illusions that we would see each and every kid accept the message that we had for them about freedom in Christ. We also knew that many would get along in their lives and away from the Ranch and the truth planted during that time there would find fertile soil in their souls and germinate into the life changes that result from acceptance. I was to find out in the years that followed that very thing did indeed happen for many of the kids we loved there. I treasure the calls and Facebook connections that have been made with them since we have left. I am blessed immeasurably to have a small spot in their lives to peek in and see how the mighty hand of

God has worked and continues to work in them and their families.

Chapter Fourteen – Oh So High A Price

We were getting so very tired as the end of the third year and beginning of the fourth arrived. We knew we needed to get away and rest and so we did get a few days off at Christmas time. The girls left on Ranch would go to the boys Ranch and spend time with the relief house parents Darryl and Diana. They were a neat couple from Colorado who followed the Lord's leading to come to Stormharbor and be relief parents for the boys' homes. We came to know them and love them as dear friends and fellow lovers of kids! They brought a unique perspective as Darryl had worked with at risk kids back in Colorado.

We went to Branson, Missouri to a timeshare condo which was made available in the off season for the staff of Stormharbor. We did not realize until that time, how far down we had gotten physically, emotionally, and spiritually. We had passed the national average of 9-18 months that a houseparent usually lasts. We needed respite and thought that after six months of doing other jobs on Ranch we would be ready to parent again, or to go ahead and develop more homes for Serenity Valley. We talked and prayed and slept during our time there. We composed a letter to the director laying out all the different things we could do to "earn our keep" and help the Ranch. Bill had run a multimillion dollar company and brought it back from some difficult times. He had also been head of operations at this company and knew how to organize and administer programs that would develop the Ranch and help in this business side. I taught piano, voice, and wrote grants in my other life and had those skills to bring to the table as well. We could relief for the houseparents of girls or boys. We saw that there was much we could do and still contribute to the welfare of the kids and the Ranch. We were willing to go and speak to churches about Serenity Valley, hoping to garner support for building more houses there and taking more girls. We felt that we had been trained well and could help with new houseparents just getting started in taking care of at risk girls. Overall we believed that we were still on track to fulfill the promises made to us before we left Michigan. We would house parent for a time and then step into the role of administrators of the girl's ranch. We had no reason to believe otherwise. We finished our time there and came home. Bill was unsettled about the letter feeling that we were not going to see the outcome that we wanted. He had been feeling for a long time like we were being used up and were going to be thrown away. I could not find it in my heart to believe that would be the outcome. Surely they know that we had been "all in" at Serenity Valley, surely God would provide and protect us from harm. Surely they would see what an asset we had become to the ministry, we had sacrificed so very much. They had sent us to great training and invested in us and Serenity Valley. Surely it was not expendable, we were not expendable. We had used up our retirement to build and repair and take care of the kids. We had used up ourselves as well. We just needed to rest and then everything would go back to normal. We had a full house of girls and they needed us. We told them we would house parent until June. One of our girls who had been there a long time was leaving in June it would make a good break point for us to step back. We were not leaving ranch so the kids would still be in our lives, just in a different capacity. We could still be a part of their daily lives just in a different capacity.

   Things on Ranch had deteriorated financially and the economy was suffering. The stock market had nearly crashed and with it our monies in our IRA. We were told we could look forward to retiring and living there on Ranch. We could put a mobile home on the property and be a part of Ranch life in our retirement years. We believed that and welcomed the time ahead as we saw the Lord continue to work in the lives of the kids who came down the Stormharbor road. We had seen the Lord move in so many amazing ways and kids whose lives were shattered begin the healing process that would lead to a life of peace and fulfillment in Christ. We had laughed and cried, and laughed some more. We were seasoned in our lives and our marriage. We knew that Stormharbor would exact a cost and were willing to pay it. We had made sweet and loving friends and found betrayal by others. We had much left to give and were willing to do what it took to remain a part of the Ranch community. We still had a daughter and son- in- law and our first grandson on Ranch. We had a church family in Hot Springs that we loved, we have been supported and cared for by our church family in Michigan. We had kept many up to date with newsletters and visits. We believed we were right in the center of God's will being there and serving our girls. We could not envision anywhere else we would rather be.

We waited a week for an answer from the director about our proposal. We knew that either way nothing would change for at least six months so we pushed ahead taking care of Serenity Valley and the girls. Finally we were asked if we could have a meeting with the director of homes and the ranch director one Friday afternoon. We agreed, we were anxious that it had taken so very long to address the requests in the letter.

We were called later, and the meeting was cancelled and had to be rescheduled. We were again wondering what the future would hold for us, and the girls at Serenity Valley. There had been so many good times, and hard times, at the Lodge at Serenity Valley. We had poured ourselves out to serve Christ as we knew how. We had seen many lives changed and healing started. Now we were on the edge, hoping and praying for a chance to rest and heal up and begin again the mission to help hurting kids. The meeting was scheduled for Friday afternoon, and we came early, anxious to hear what the next step would be. Bill was quiet and tense; he knew that it could end up differently than we wanted. We knew there were many who did not want Serenity Valley, and the program there, to happen in the first place. We also knew that some thought that Serenity Valley would take away funding that could keep Shiloh Valley going. They did not want brash Yankees coming in and telling them what to do, and what to think. We were totally unaware of these feelings for years, but slowly, as money got tighter and folks got stretched, we heard the rumblings about Serenity Valley. Many did not know what we had sacrificed, it was not important in the eternal scheme of things. God knows, and He will be the judge of the thoughts and intents of our hearts.

We went in and sat down in the Director's office. As I said before, also present was the Director of Homes. We asked if they had read the proposal, and what they thought of it all. The Director was silent, and the Director of Homes said that, in his experience, when houseparent's are tired they just need to be let go. We had six weeks to pack up our stuff and leave the ranch. I could not believe what we had just heard. I was in shock. The Director said they needed houseparent's, and that the board wanted them to spend their money on filling that position. I could not process what was happening. The Director sat silent, and the Director of Homes said that they would follow us back to Serenity Valley to break the news to the girls. It was supper time, and we arrived to find them setting the table and getting ready. We were still reeling when Bill told the girls we would no longer be their houseparent's after the weekend was over. There was shock, and many started to cry. One of our youngest girls said that Bill was her Dad, to which the Director of Homes said she could have another one. He laughed, they did not. I was crying and Bill was crying. They left us after that--with a house full of upset kids. It was Friday night, and we were on duty all weekend. Not once during that time did anyone from the administrative staff call to check on us, or come over. Our own family came to our aide, and stayed with us through that whole time. On Monday morning we were home and watched the girls leave for school with our RI. I had not slept well at all that night, and had talked and cried and prayed. We needed answers to how we ended up with this happening. I can tell you that God did comfort us, as did most of the folks at our church in Hot Springs.

That Monday morning I was standing in the kitchen of our house and the phone rang. The Director asked to speak with us. I requested that he come over to Serenity Valley. In the meantime, Bill had come into the kitchen and he said, "Cindi, I have been up all night and I know that God does not want us to stay here. We cannot trust the administration to keep their word, and we need to leave as soon as possible." We did not have the funds to move, we did not own a vehicle as we had donated ours to a ministry when we left Michigan because we were provided Ranch vehicles to drive. We did not know where we would go, and yet God had a plan in place already. Our daughter and son-in-law, who lived in a nearby town, called and said for us to put our stuff in storage and move in with them until we were rested and had clear leading as to where God wanted us to go next. I could not conceive of leaving behind all that we had accomplished at Serenity Valley. It was, however, just a piece of ground--and God had started the work there and would finish it.

The Director came over, and was sad and quiet. He had not slept that night much, either, and had said that he would find a way for us to stay. We declined his offer. We asked for severance, and a vehicle, and the ability to keep a dentist appointment that the Ranch was to help pay for. He agreed to all that. We prayed and he left. We moved ahead to get the process started of moving from the Ranch—leaving behind our dreams for Serenity Valley. There were many tears shed, and there were hard feelings. I was called out for grieving, and told that was wrong. To this day, I do not know how many truly understood what had happened, God does, and that's enough for me.

We moved from Serenity Valley six weeks almost to the day from the day we were let go. The boys came over and helped us pack the truck. I was very sad that we did not see more of the staff, with whom we had lived and worked, come and say good bye. They had a "memorial" one night at chapel in our honor. It was very difficult to sit and listen to the accolades. We loved the girls, and missed them so very much.

It was better for them that we were gone, then they could begin to put their lives back on track again. They had new house parents, and would have to learn the way they wanted things to run in the house. I looked back one more time as we pulled out of Serenity Valley. I saw the beautiful crepe myrtles that would bloom in the summer and fill the circle drive with glorious color. The flower beds would be awash with day lilies, and roses, and azaleas. The dreams we had for a place that was safe and secure and peaceful for girls to come to and find Jesus Christ and healing were now gone. We had poured our hearts into that valley, and we were leaving with them bruised and weary.

Chapter Fifteen – Life after Serenity Valley

No, that is not the end of the story. The truth is that often Christians shoot their wounded. We are the ones who hurt others who are laboring in the trenches right beside us. We have lost the example that Christ set—to love one another as He has loved us.

We moved in with our kids, and spent some quality time with our small grandson, daughter, and "son-in-love." They had announced that they were going to begin the process of leaving the states to go to the mission field. We tried to make the most of every moment without getting into each other's hair. God showed up, over and over, in His care and love of us all. We knew we were not done in service yet, but we were raw and wary of putting our lives on the line in another place. The girls will never know how much we loved them, and how deeply we missed being there as a part of their lives. One graduated from high school, and we did go back to the Ranch to honor her and the accomplishments she had achieved. It was painful and awkward. Everyone there was led to believe that we decided on our own to leave, and that it was for our health. That is as good a "spin" as any, as to why we had decided not to stay. God would take care of the details.

We responded to this event by going through the grieving process. The death of hopes and dreams, the physical, mental, emotional and spiritual depletion, were all key factors in what we experienced. In the years since we left the Ranch, I have spoken too many who were in ministry and found the same story repeated over and over again. We use up our pastors and missionaries, and expect that those in ministry should joyfully live in poverty while their families make huge sacrifices. This mindset is flawed. We should whole-heartedly support those who go and serve. You are called one of two ways--either you go or you support those who do. You don't pat them on the back, then forget they exist until you have a need. We are, indeed, a team--the "Body of Christ" on this earth. We should not use the worldly model of doing things. Instead, we should function within the confines of the Word of God. We learned many lessons, and this was just one.

If we go back to a Biblical example during the ministry of Christ here on the earth, he would get away from the crowd and his disciples, rest, and talk to His heavenly Father. There is a saying that I have heard many times and it goes like this, "If a Christian does not '"come apart"', he will come apart." In the world of child care workers in ministry, there is a huge deficit in what they are paid compared to their secular counterparts. They are often living below the poverty level, and many have to go to the state for assistance to meet the basic needs that they have. The church in America does not step in to see to the needs of its ministry staff. It is on the church to take better care of their staff.

We did not do everything right. We made mistakes. We knew, though, that God would meet our needs--and He did. There were a number of times we needed help, and right on time it arrived. There were times of fellowship and joy, there were also landmarks of healing that came as each girl began to trust and accept her placement. There was laughter and love. These were all blessings that we received as a result of our time at Serenity Valley. Our hearts were changed and we were not the same two people who drove that U-Haul truck down into Serenity Valley in January of 2006. God still had a plan, even if we did not know what it was. We were now 54 and 55 years old. We knew that getting employment was going to be difficult, and we were prepared to be disappointed. God was, however, already paving the way for us, and preparing a place for us to serve Him next.

As I mentioned before, our son-in-law was an associate pastor at a church in Russellville, and they had stayed at a place called Oaks Manor Conference and Retreat Center. He heard that the director's wife had passed away the previous year, and the director was managing with volunteers to keep the Retreat Center going. We had stayed at their cottage a few times as well, free of charge as it is there for those in ministry to get away and rest. I called him to ask if he needed any help, and to tell him we had left the Ranch--and the circumstances of our exit. He was so excited, and asked us to come and visit the next weekend, and attend the Board of Directors meeting. We agreed, and went, not knowing what to expect. They unanimously invited us to join the ministry staff there, and we accepted. We were excited to begin this new chapter in our lives, God had sent a lifeboat along--in His time. We were to start on April 1, and had a few weeks before we were to be there so we took a trip to Florida to visit my mother and see friends who were wintering there. We came back ready to move again into the apartment at the Manor House, and start our new life there. I will save the story of our time there for another book. Suffice to say that God did show up and take care of us. We have learned some painful lessons, and had great blessings and joy as well. We met and loved so many girls, and were able to give them the place to rest and heal. We know now that God accomplished exactly what He wanted to there, and we were blessed and humbled to be a part of it.

    They moved the girls out of the valley, and to the boy's ranch. For a time there were boys living at Serenity Valley, and then they were moved back. We heard that they eventually sold Serenity Valley. We were so sad to hear that, however Serenity Valley lives on in the hearts of those girls who found a home there--and it lives on in our hearts too. It was the symbol of two people leaving all that they knew behind in order to be obedient to a call God placed on their lives to serve Him by serving wounded girls.

    My kids asked me recently why I was writing this book, what I wanted to see happen as a result of my having it published. First and foremost, I wanted to give all the glory to my Lord and Savior Jesus Christ. He alone led us through our time at Serenity Valley. He alone gave us the strength and wisdom, peace, joy, and laughter we experienced. He engineered the setting for us to see the need in our lives to heal from past hurts. Our marriage is stronger than it had ever been, and we are more committed to each other. We have fallen deeper in love, and it was a wonderment to us both. Our family had grown--we have five grand babies!! What a joy to be present for their births. What a blessing to work side-by-side with our kids and their spouses, serving the Lord we all dearly love. We had been present for the beginning of a new time of ministry, and had been able to put our love and care into the facility to see it bloom and grow. We were welcomed by amazing Christians into a fellowship in Hot Springs. They loved on us, and the girls we brought to church, and they participated in the ministry through prayer, and through running a camp that our kids were welcomed to participate in. We also spent a time worshipping in Perryville at the First Baptist Church there. They were sweet and welcoming as well. We were privileged to come to know and love many of the staff, and to call them friends. Many of those friendships last to this day, even though we are miles apart from each other. Bonds formed in the trenches of spiritual warfare are often the sweetest and deepest. I know that we did not always see eye-to-eye, and we were even judgmental and harsh with each other. I wanted there to be forgiveness and reconciliation as soon as possible, because I loved them and wanted to be in right standing with them.

If you decide to go into ministry, you must use due diligence when you are planning that move. Research the programming and the staff. Ask to see the finances. Financial information should be transparent--where anyone can see what is taking place there. Pray—and pray—and pray some more. Get the names of those who have served and left, and hear their stories. This all should be freely given to you. If there is reluctance, then you must ask yourself why. You are leaving all behind to serve, so be sure that they believe in the same doctrinal principles that you do. Finding deep difference can lead to strife, and maybe even having to leave your post.

Make sure that they can, and will, support you. If you need to raise some support on your own make sure that that your supporters understand that their donations to the ministry may or may not be allocated to you in the end. If it is possible, spend time there just to see how things are done, and see the daily commitments that will be required of you. You can never find out everything, and there is the element of trust that comes as a result of your call. Remember that there are so many places you can serve. You must find one that takes care of their staff as if they were a precious commodity. If there is a large staff turnover you might want to step back and seek God for His wisdom and leading before you join. Use great wisdom with your personal finances when you join a ministry that is struggling financially. You will find yourself giving of your assets in order to take care of the things that have fallen through the cracks. Please be smart about keeping your personal funds separate from the ministry.

There is much to be said for the experience of serving Christ on the front line, where it matters if you show up day-to-day. We have been seasoned now from our time in the front lines. We have experience and the hind sight that comes from that. God has seen fit to leave us here on this earth for now, and we are blessed to be used whenever He sees fit.

One of the greatest joys of my life was rearing our two girls, as well as having the five years with our son. I am a mother in my heart, and know that it was, and still is, my greatest accomplishment in life. I was filled up with love and laughter houseparenting the girls of Serenity Valley. They know that we were there for them, to care for them, to laugh with them, to teach them life lessons, and finally to lead them to the Savior. I am confident to this day that we were successful for the most part. They are all young women now, some married with children of their own, some not. Wherever they are, and whatever they are doing, I still pray for them, wanting them to have all that our Savior has in store for them. I want them to have peace and joy in their lives, and to grow up spiritually in the Lord. That is all we ever wanted from the first day to the last.

We are not saints, and we did battle for a time with hurt, anger, and feelings of betrayal. Those are huge deep raw emotions that needed healing. Now we are both at peace, knowing that where we are now is just where God wants us to be. We hope and pray that in the future we will again be able to live in the Ozark Mountains. We fell in love with the northwest corner of Arkansas. It is breathtakingly beautiful. We have family still in the state, and want to someday move back closer to them to live. I still have a dream to buy a big old house, and restore it as a retreat for those in ministry who have been wounded and burned out. I want it to be a place to pour love and care into their lives for a time, then hopefully send them back into the battle for souls that rages on in our country.

I know our time to parent at risk teens is over. Bill has suffered much damage to his body from the long hours of physical labor needed to keep things running. He is now sixty, and I am fifty nine, and we have lived three lives in the past nine years. We know that season in our lives is done. However, if you live close to a facility, you can be a foster grandparent. There is a huge need for that role played by Godly folks. We saw what an impact that made in the lives of our kids. They felt special when older folks would listen to them, and love on them. The houseparent's would welcome the help I am sure.

We can now stand before the throne of God, bow, and say we answered His call to serve, and we laid it all on the line for those wonderful girls of Serenity Valley. Being Mom and Dad for them was a joy that we could never have imagined, and for many of them that is who we still are. What a blessing, what an adventure in faith, what a legacy to leave in honor of the King of Kings and Lord of Lords, Jesus Christ.

I wanted to say "Thank You!" from the bottom of my heart to my daughter Leigh Ann and her husband Jeff, and to our daughter Meredith and her husband Amos. They were there to pick up the pieces, give us sanctuary, and love when we were so very wounded. They have walked all the way through with us. We are humbled to be so blessed with the greatest family one could ask for. In life, we rarely get to see the hand of God work and change lives. We were blessed to be on the front lines for so many of those events. We know that if there is never another opportunity to serve kids we will be sad, and yet know that we answered God's call and were blessed beyond measure as a result.

As I sat on the front porch of the Lodge at Serenity Valley, I prayed that God would see fit to use me for His purposes. He answered that prayer, and took Bill and me to places we could never have imagined in our wildest dreams. We lived in the beauty of the Ouachita Mountains, we saw the beauty in the wildness of the country that surrounded us, yet we were secure and safe in the center of God's will. I will always love Serenity Valley. The place is just ground, but the work that God did in our lives and the lives of all those girls was a miracle of immense proportions. God showed up each and every day that we were there. He held us up through some very deep and painful times, and He showed up in the laughter, and hugs and love that was everywhere when you have girls who finally trust in His love. I have a friend who is still on staff there, and she was, for me, a sounding board, a coach, a counselor, and most of all a sister in Christ. She walked with me through some very deep waters, she shared her heart and her wisdom, and we laughed many times together. I know that she heard my heart many times when I could not express my pain with words. She will always have a place in my heart and I pray for her as she continues on to this day doing what she can to comfort, and love on, girls and boys who have been wounded and need a safe place to be.

You see, there are warriors in many facilities all across this vast country of ours--people who are daily on the front lines, fighting to bring kids back to a place where they can meet Jesus Christ and be healed. Many places are inner city, and they are working tirelessly to provide a safe place, a meal, clothes, and love to kids who are on the streets, who have been kicked out of their homes, or who have run away to escape the abuse. There are people there, fighting the good fight to stand in the gap and reach a hand out to say, "Come with me and find rest."

In repentance and rest you shall be saved, in quietness and confidence is your strength. Therefore the Lord longs to be gracious to you and therefore He waits on high to have compassion on you. - Isaiah 30:15, 18

Is it so amazing that God would call us from all that we knew and loved, to go and serve Him? Has He been calling you? Can you walk away from all you know to start an adventure that will most surely bring about a total transformation in your heart and life? I think if you examine your heart you will know that God has called you, maybe not to leave your country, state or city, but maybe to step beyond all that you find comfortable and safe. Maybe you are called to volunteer in the inner city, or at a homeless shelter, or at a hospital. Where can you become Jesus Christ's hands and feet in this dying world? When you arrive in heaven will you be missing someone because you did not speak to him about the Lord?

The challenge has not changed in centuries....

The Spirit of the Lord is on me, because he has anointed me to proclaim good news to the poor. He has sent me to proclaim freedom for the prisoners and recovery of sight for the blind, to set the oppressed free... - Luke 4:18

We have the keys to the kingdom placed in our hands by the finished work of Jesus Christ on the Cross of Calvary, followed by the immeasurable power of the resurrection. Can you keep silent? How much time will we have to reach into the lives of these young men and women? Will you step out in faith and trust God to hold you as you start one of the greatest adventures you will ever have this side of heaven?

I pray that you will.

Appendix

Girls Lodge

Bunk House – Tucker Residence

Bill & Cindi Tucker

WHERE COURTESY FAILS, RULES PREVAIL

Meaning: Laws(rules)are created when humans fail to treat each other and themselves with respect and dignity. So to help Bill and Cindi be House Parents not House Police:

Prevent a sister from making a mistake. Let a staff person or house parent know of any problems, conflicts, and unapproved plans. Your knowledge makes you a responsible party.

Come tell us immediately of problems and mistakes, do not wait to get caught! We are here to help you learn how to make better decisions in the future.

Feel sorrow for others when they make a mistake. Ask yourself this question—"How would I want to be treated when I make a mistake?"

Talk with us privately to resolve conflicts (instead of battling it out with each other), so that necessary corrections can be made to keep everyone advancing in privileges and goals (return home, get an education, go to college, get a good job....etc.)

Hug Bill, Cindi and Tanya often, if you can. We are people who love to hug but if it makes you uncomfortable, we will not touch you. We love, and care for all of our girls. Hugs merely are a show of affection, not a measure of our love.

Help make this house a home, safe and loving for all that live here and visit.

Take care of the house, its contents, and your belongings.

Respect the privacy of others and ask permission from staff before borrowing anything.

Complete all your chores without supervision and look around to see if something else needs to be done.

Serenity Valley Ranch Creed

Made in the USA
Lexington, KY
02 May 2016